LR/LEND/001

PORNOGRAPHY AND THE SEX CRISIS

For Molly Simone,
my daily reminder that change is necessary and possible.

PORNOGRAPHY AND THE SEX CRISIS

by

SUSAN G. COLE

Introduction by
SHEILA JEFFREYS

UNIVERSITY OF WOLVERHAMPTON
LIBRARY

Acc No.	CLASS	
2160358	363·	
CONTROL	47	
0921299060		
DATE	SITE	COL
-8 MAR 1999	Dy	

AN AMANITA PUBLICATION

CANADIAN CATALOGUING IN PUBLICATION DATA

Cole, Susan G., 1952-
Pornography and the sex crisis
Includes bibliographical references.

1. Pornography—Social aspects. I.Title
HQ471.C64   1989   363.4'7   C89-093460-6

Copyright© 1989 by Susan G. Cole

Cover and Book Design by Elizabeth Martin
Typesetting by Third Generation Graphics Ltd.
Manuscript preparation by Facilities for Writers
Printing by Metropole Litho Inc., Quebec
Amanita Logo Design by Dougal Haggart

PRINTED AND BOUND IN CANADA

ORDER INFORMATION:

Amanita Enterprises
PO Box 784, Station P
Toronto, Ontario, Canada
M5S 2Z1

CONTENTS

PREFACE

In 1978, I had the good fortune to meet Tatiana Mamanova, a Soviet feminist who had been expelled from the USSR for subversive political activities. She had spent a little less than a year in Paris before touring North America to promote a publication of writings from the Soviet feminist movement. I remember her as wary and not yet sure who to trust. She was definitely a regretful exile, and not at all one of the fortune hunters who fled the Soviet Union gleefully anticipating an orgy of materialism. It was her healthy ambivalence toward both sides of the Iron Curtain that made me want to hear more from her.

As we were talking about the political movement of artists in her country of exile, about how difficult it was to organize in the USSR, and about how violence against women was epidemic there just as it is here in the west, I quite suddenly asked her what difference she had noticed first in the west. "The pornography," she said immediately. "It's everywhere, even on billboards."

I pressed her. We had just been talking about wife assault, as prevalent as ever in the Soviet Union, even without visible pornography. "Yes, but this is a different kind of assault. And it doesn't feel like freedom to me."

The conversation was the second of two powerful experiences that convinced me to write a book about pornography. The first occurred the year before, when the film *Snuff* arrived in a Toronto theatre. *Snuff* was a repulsive shred of celluloid which, its producers claimed, featured the real murder of a real woman as sexually titillating entertainment. The presence of *Snuff* enraged some women so completely that they shut down the theatre one night in a direct — and spontaneous — political action. The incident turned into a media event and for days after, women from all over the city came downtown to the Yonge Street "strip" to protest outside the theatre. The diversity of the protesters was astonishing.

I became aware then that pornography was an issue that could really move people. But I learned quickly that the people organizing against pornography's proliferation do not have a monopoly on passion. The defenders of pornography, as well as those who think pornography is awful but that censorship is worse, have charged the issue with the kind of emotional energy that may be unparalleled in the history of the feminist movement. As a result, the debates on pornography and sexuality have been angry and bitter.

It was women's rights lawyer Mary Eberts who remarked that pornography was the women's movement's Skokie. The divisions generated by the debate reminded her of the way the American Jewish community was torn apart when prominent Jewish liberals supported the right of neo-Nazis to demonstrate through the town of Skokie, Illinois. The fascist contingent had chosen Skokie because many of the town's residents were survivors of the Holocaust. Observers of the American melting pot have suggested that after Skokie, the Jewish community would never again know the solidarity it had found in the postwar period. In the same way, chroniclers of the feminist movement have contended that the movement would never be the same after the bitterness of the pornography debates.

The bitterness created an environment in which the substance of the arguments has not been fully registered. Some women fighting pornography stereotype anti-censorship feminists as uncaring about pornography and violence against women. Angry anti-censorship activists still imagine that all feminists who hate pornography love censorship. For my own part, I have been frustrated by encounters in which hostile questioners have attributed to me ideas that have nothing to do with my thinking. That is why I am so excited about the publication of this book. To my knowledge, this is the first radical feminist book on pornography published in Canada. Now I can write it exactly as I see it.

Nevertheless, there will be women who refuse to recognize the situations of physical and emotional pain that I describe in this text. They will say they have never experienced discrimination, that they could fend off a sexual assailant, that they have made successes of themselves because of their own talent and not because a movement of political women paved the way. They may read this book and say, "This is all about losers and I am a winner." I hope these readers will listen to the voices of women whose lives have been devastated by the institution of pornography, and I hope readers will understand that knowing these things have not happened to them will not take away the pain from the women who have suffered. It also will not guarantee that these things will *not* happen to them, or their loved ones, some time in the future.

Because of sensitivities about the topic, I have tried to be very careful about my use of the word feminist. This text provides a feminist view of pornography. It is not *the* feminist view. I do not believe I can appropriate all of feminism when it comes to my views on pornography. On the other hand, I do not think the word feminism is so vague that it always has to be used with qualifiers — as in liberal feminist, socialist feminist, lesbian feminist or the term radical feminist, which I use to describe myself. I *do* think the word feminism has some meaning and carries with it some political bottom lines. So, when I refer to the struggle for women's equality, I call it feminist. When I refer to the battle for women's reproductive rights, I call it feminist as well. But when I describe feminists fighting censorship I call them anti-censorship feminists, and when I describe feminists like myself who are fighting pornography, I use the term anti-pornography feminists.

This book is divided into three chapters. The first sets up the theoretical framework for understanding what pornography is and does. What I have learned is that pornography is not a picture, or words or ideas, but a practice of sexual subordination in which women's inferior status is eroticized and thus maintained. The analysis takes into account the experiences of women who are in the pornography, the stereotypes pornography promotes, and the way they have made their way into the cultural mainstream.

On this note I should add that although sexual subordination is a cross-cultural phenomenon, this book does not offer a world-wide perspective. Because of my own interest in mass media, and because the pornography produced in North America is infamous for its violent character, I have focussed my explorations on this continent, and broaden the discussion at most to the industrialized west.

The first chapter goes on to deal with the impact of pornography on consumers, on the women around them and on society in general. Here it's pertinent to comment on the use of the social science research that I refer to support some of my views. There are wildly divergent opinions on the usefulness of the clinical research. I have met people who insist that science does leave us with the last word, and others who scoff at these studies, claiming they are more fiction than science.

I confess to my own ambivalance about the data. My problem with the research centres around the breathtaking silence of women in the laboratory. I have never really felt that women needed a patriarch in a lab coat to tell us what rape feels like, or whether pornography feels like assault. The fact that researchers have almost always examined male responses to pornography has convinced me that women's reactions to pornography are not taken all that seriously in the scientific community. I have tried to reverse the research trend with my own pornography study, which I also describe in this chapter. But I offer the clinical data here as a response to anyone, especially policy-makers, who wants this specific kind of scientific "proof" before they can be convinced to take action. Where possible I've used the endnotes to describe the methodologies of researchers. I suggest that the clinical research is at least as strong as the data on the harms of tobacco.

The first chapter ends with a description of the changing landscape of the pornography debate and the way the analysis of pornography offered here differs from the traditional moralist opposition. The section also describes the way anti-pornography perspectives cut through the traditional political dichotomies of right and left and the law's arbitrary division of public and private.

The second chapter is about the law, its limitations and its possibilities for fighting pornography. The analysis establishes seven feminist criteria for anti-pornography law and uses them to measure the existing legal machinery that supposedly deals with pornography. It goes on to recommend a specific and narrow legal strategy designed to provide some remedy for the actual harm of pornography and to compensate victims. This civil remedy provides the only instance in which I think the state should be encouraged to intervene. My critiques of mass media and sexuality do not carry a legal agenda.

The third and final chapter begins a radical analysis of sexuality, locating pornography in a process through which sexuality is socially constructed to reinforce male power and female powerlessness. This sex-critical perspective challenges the moralist, liberal and liberationist stances that have dominated the discourse on sexuality throughout this century (my review of the sex liberal text *Women Against Censorship* is reprinted as an appendix), and identifies a sex crisis so profound that it must be put on the social agenda. I have offered a few ideas about how we can face the crisis, but the movement to counter the sexual ideology of male dominance and female submission has only taken its very first breaths. It needs nurturing, intelligence and a new kind of passion.

This book is the product of ten years of political action and thought. The period of gestation was so long because pornography wound up being the issue through which I became radicalized; or, as I used to say to anybody who wondered about the manuscript: the ideas just would not stay still. Throughout the decade, scores of supporters have given encouragement to me and clarity to my ideas. I cannot mention them all but I would like to give some special thanks, beginning with a number of organizations: the Ontario Women's Directorate, the Canada Council, the Ontario Arts Council and the Metro Action Committee on Public Violence Against Women and Children, for funding along the way; to the Civil Rights and Remedies Committee for their commitment; and to the *Broadside* collective for giving me a voice.

I also want to express my deep appreciation to all the women who courageously shared their experience; to Brettel Dawson, Mary Lou Fassel and Sheila McIntyre for their warm support and legal expertise; to Jane Farrow and Wendy Wine for primary research pursued with wonderful enthusiasm; to Catharine

MacKinnon and Andrea Dworkin for inspiration; to Ted Mumford for his intelligent and sensitive handling of the manuscript; to Lisa Freedman, Susan Crean, Lynne Fernie, Diana Majury and Darlene Lawson for the depth of their friendship; to my publisher and long-time friend Eve Zaremba, who was convinced that there was a book there somewhere and who wouldn't let me flit down my freelance path until it was complete; and, finally, to my partner Leslie Chud for all of her light.

Susan G. Cole
Toronto
January 1989

INTRODUCTION

IT GIVES ME CONSIDERABLE PLEASURE to be able to introduce Susan Cole's book. Cole offers not simply lucid feminist analysis of pornography and some strategies for dealing with it, but a way to understand the massive backlash that has been organized against the feminist challenge. This is the direction in which feminist theory must develop in future. Cole explains the backlash by looking at what she calls the "sex crisis." The crusade to defend pornography is shown here in the context of the way sex is thought about and experienced under male supremacy. Pornography, as she explains, does real harm to women, both those used in the production of pornography and those who suffer through men's use of it. Yet the harm of pornography is nearly invisible to the pornbrokers, the civil libertarians who defend it and the sexual libertarians who are keen to use pornography and to make it their own. Susan Cole helps us to understand this puzzle.

It is difficult at first to understand why pornography should be defended in a way that other discriminatory depictions of women are not. Pornography, as Cole makes clear, is an abusive practice, but it is also a form of sex-stereotyping. Women are routinely shown as passive and submissive objects who desire abuse, even in some cases unto death. Other forms of sexist stereotyping of women and girls in the media have been successfully campaigned against by feminists in this wave of feminism. In Britain the Campaign Against Sex Stereotyping in Education sought to get rid of damaging stereotypes in school textbooks. School texts which always showed Janet in an apron helping mommy at the sink and John under a car with daddy were criticized and banished from many schools. Now anti-sexist education committees scrutinize library books for such overt sexism. There are no howls of protest. Even when campaigns against sexist stereotyping began to include materials for adults, the civil libertarians did not seek to protect freedom of speech. Yet as soon as feminist organizations were set up to fight pornography in Britain, and elsewhere, the anti-censorship lobby stepped into the fray. Feminists were told that any challenge to pornography threatened civil liberties and particularly freedom of speech. This was long before any legal remedies were suggested, and was clearly not really motivated by concern about censorship. Susan Cole discusses various legal remedies which could be used against the damage done to women in the making of pornography and in its use, and explains why the fierce campaign that has been organiz- ed against such initiatives, again in the name of anti-censorship, has been misguided.

So why did any public criticism of pornography or picketing of pornbrokers arouse such a furore, summoning the sleeping giants of sexual liberalism to the battlements when criticism of other forms of sex-stereotyping in the media did not? Sex is seen as a special case. This is because, as U.S. campaigners against por- nography such as Catharine MacKinnon have pointed out, that which is recognized as sex under male supremacy is precisely the sexualized inequality of women. This kind of sex has a crucial political function. Sexologists throughout this century have argued that men should and do strengthen their "masculinity," i.e., dominance, through doing sex. They have argued that women must be trained to experience adequate sexual response since this response would both require and effect their submission, not just in the bedroom but in the whole relationship and in the world outside the bedroom. In twentieth-century male supremacy, a whole industry has developed to train us in dominance and sub- mission sex. Sex, it seems, is not the innocent garden of delights that we have been encouraged to believe it to be. And por- nography shows this most graphically.

Defenders of pornography are very often defending the degradation of women in pornography because that is what turns them on. In a society in which both men and women have been trained — particularly those of us who experienced the "sexual revolution" — to see sexual pleasure as the ultimate form of individual fulfillment, people are understandably anxious to have their share. This can appear to require the defence of pornography or the values it promotes. But those who experience a sexual response to pornography do not necessarily feel the need to defend it. It can be devastating to recognize that the degradation of women is a turn-on, but the anger this recognition can arouse, when directed against the pornbrokers and the male power they uphold, should be a motivating force in our struggle. Unfortunately too often this anger is actually turned against anti-pornography feminists. Some who are aroused by pornography see any challenge to it as an attempt to take sex away from them. An alternative form of sex, an eroticized mutuality and equality, is almost unimaginable. Anti-pornography campaigners are demanding a total transformation of the way "sex" is learned and experienced. Such a profound change is integral to women's liberation. This is an unacceptable demand to many and has resulted in what Susan Cole identifies as the "sex crisis." Those who wish to continue to use the subordination of women as the wellspring of their pleasures and satisfaction are now standing in the road and trying to bring the progress of feminist revolution to a halt.

We can see now why pornography has become such a controversial issue and why sex is seen as a special case, a protected area of discrimination. In a society in which it is unfashionable to promote the economic subordination of women, the abuse of women in pornography is seen as just "sex." Sex is the last bastion. It is protected because it provides a big game reserve in which men may still legitimately hunt women even though in the world outside they must pay lip service to equality of opportunity. The battle that has developed around pornography between feminists and sexual libertarians testifies to the poignancy of the "sex crisis." The question at issue is just how much liberation women are to be allowed. Feminists cannot allow sex to remain a protected area of women's oppression in order to protect the sexual satisfactions that this can afford. In *Pornography and the*

Sex Crisis Susan Cole demystifies the so-called debate which has been taking place around pornography and ends by being optimistic about the creation of a new kind of sex, an eroticized equality, to resolve the sex crisis.

Sheila Jeffreys
London, UK
January 1989

SHEILA JEFFREYS is the author of *The Spinster and Her Enemies: Feminism and Sexuality 1880-1930*.

CHAPTER I

PORNOGRAPHY

1

LESS THAN TWENTY YEARS AGO, before feminists gave the issue any attention, there were only three actors involved in the pornography debate. The first, the agent of liberation, was the pornographer. According to him, pornography was the passport to a life of sensuality, free of constraints, prejudice and authority. The second, the agent of repression, represented the moralist forces defending the family and religious values. He considered pornography a threat to a man's husbandly duty, and held that pornography both chained men to their physical needs and liberated a sexual drive that was dangerous to society. These combatants had long fought over the right of the third actor, the consumer, to stimulate his sexual appetites.

Feminists noticed that this happy triumvirate of pornographer, moralist and consumer misses something: women. It leaves out the women involved with the consumers; it leaves out the women who are in the actual pictures and words of pornography; and it leaves out the women who believe that the pervasiveness of pornography has an impact on their lives. No wonder the feminist perspectives on pornography, when they finally appeared, were so misrepresented and misunderstood. It is hard to redefine a discourse that has been so closed for so long. It has always been hard to make women's voices heard.

This book puts women first and takes them seriously, and refuses to let the male view remain the only view. It analyzes pornography in a way that does not allow the debate to be reduced to the question, "Are you for pornography or against it." Rather it demands that pornography be redefined, and re-examined in a clearer light.

It also insists on asking questions about pornography that were never asked in the traditional discourse, questions like: Who are the women in pornography? How do they get there? Would you feel comfortable removing your clothes for money? Would you have sex for money? What does pornography do to women's status in society? How does it influence society's image of women? What kind of barriers does pornography pose to women's equality rights?

Two basic principles underlie the analysis of pornography in this book. The first is that women matter, and an analysis of pornography that does not take women into account is badly skewed. Second, pornography is not just a picture, a two-dimensional artifact or an idea. It is a practice[1] consisting of specific activities performed by real people. The notion that pornography is a practice helps do away with the issues of taste, interpretation and offended sensibilities that muddy the debate on pornography, and it gets at the crucial issue of who is doing what to whom. Defining pornography as a practice and not as a picture transforms the way pornography is discussed. Instead of asking "does pornography cause violence?", we discover that women are abused to make the materials that (male) consumers use in ways that are abusive to women. Abuse is not *caused* by pornography, it is part of what pornography *is*. Through this perspective the linear argument of cause and effect gives way to the description of a cycle of abuse in which pornography reinvents itself.

To get a sense of how this perspective challenges pre-existing notions of what pornography is, consider these two examples:

> You are watching a movie. On the screen, a woman is lying down on what looks like a bed, though it could be a table. A movie director filming all of this walks to the table and cuts off two of her fingers with a pair of garden shears. He then saws off her arm. Then he carves her open from the sternum to the belly and eviscerates her. The camera crew is shown becoming sexually aroused. The movie ends with the killer holding up the woman's guts triumphantly as he howls his pleasure.

> You are watching a movie. On the screen a woman is lying on a table. A doctor in uniform approaches. She takes his penis in her mouth and sucks on it, apparently greedily. He joins her on the table. She is smiling. She always smiles. He comes. So does

she, in cataclysmic tandem.

The first scene is from a movie called *Snuff*, the second from the film *Deep Throat*. Taken together, they help crystallize the conundrum facing those who try to untangle the pornography issue. Most people would agree that *Snuff* is the ultimate in pornographic excess. It turns violence into an erotic spectacle. It depicts women as dispensable objects, as things, less than human. It is no coincidence that the appearance of *Snuff* at a Toronto theatre in 1977 was a launching point for a new feminist awareness in Canada about what was happening within the pornography industry. Snuff, after all, was a fairly clear-cut case. That the producers of the film advertised the real murder of a prostitute from South America (where, the ad said, life is cheap) as the ultimate sexual turn-on made it all the more dreadful. Ultimately, the film was revealed to be an elaborate hoax — a woman was not, in fact, actually murdered, something that was obvious from a close viewing of the movie. But the deception did not eliminate any of the anger created by the film, for two reasons. First, that a woman's murder could be advertised as an erotic spectacle and attract an audience remained an outrage. Second, "snuff" movies exist as a genre. Police report that violent abusers *do* film the slow deaths of their victims.

The existence of the snuff genre and other sexually violent pornography that featured women being tortured, assaulted, cut up and maimed led some feminists to the conclusion that it wasn't the sex in pornography that was problematic, but the violence. This was too simplistic. To begin with, *Snuff* was promoted as a sexual turn-on and thus sex could not be left out of the equation. More crucially, the formulation assumed that if the pictures portrayed "just sex," then they were not pornographic or at all problematic. This brings us back to the sequence from *Deep Throat*. The movie, supposedly a comedy, is about a woman with a clitoris in her throat. What's on screen looks like fun, like sex, like consensual sex, like all the things many people might call erotica.

But the pictures do not tell the real off-screen story. In her book *Ordeal*,[2] Linda (Marchiano) Lovelace describes how she was pimped, assaulted and terrorized in the making of Deep Throat.

Her tormentor and pimp, Chuck Traynor, had "assisted" in the making of other sexually explicit movies, including a film in which Marchiano was shown accepting the sexual ministrations of a dog. She was forced to make that film at gunpoint. The gun and the assaults, however, are outside the frame of the camera.

Marchiano has had a great deal of difficulty getting people to believe her story. This poses an intriguing paradox. Viewers excuse sexual violence in pornography, assuming that it's staged. So why do they assume the "just sex" materials present women really enjoying sex? One reason viewers cannot see the harm in abusive pornographic scenarios is that the pornographer works hard to make the abuse invisible. Often, as in the case of Marchiano, the women are smiling, so that the violence suddenly looks like pleasure. That these women may have been forced to smile for these pictures is somehow not considered.

Much of the time, the violence is real in pornography. So are the women who have been bought and sold to appear in the pornography. Why then do the pictures not move observers to notice that something terrible is happening to the women shown? Perhaps the myopia has something to do with a widely shared fascination with movie magic. Moviemakers, after all, serve up fantasies and illusions, and pornography, which in 25 years has gone from 30-second black-and-white loops to full-length features with costumes and plot lines (a term used loosely here), appears to be just another movie. But the truth is that when a woman is tied up so that the ropes cut her flesh, the ropes are as tight as they appear; if a woman is beaten, there is no assurance that she is being tapped lightly and not slugged. Besides, once she is tied up, a woman has lost all immediate control of what will happen next in the production.

A film entitled *Black Emmanuelle* features the "seduction" of a black female prostitute by her pimp. The instrument of seduction is film footage of women being tortured. The women are nude, their torturers are in army fatigues. The men cut off the women's breasts, and then hang the women on meathooks so that their bodies stream with blood. Unlike *Snuff*, the brutality of *Black Emmanuelle* looks real. The scratched black-and-white film is made to look like documentary stock footage.

A film entitled *Water Power* is about a man who kills prostitutes by giving them rectal enemas. The viewer sees the rubber inserted into the woman's anus. Her pain is unmistakable. Only a profound faith in the better side of human nature can sustain the hope that these are cinematic tricks. What if it were really happening? Who would stop it? There is no union representative on the set. Can we count on the pornographer?

The pervasiveness of pornography tends to make women invisible as human beings, visible only as things or objects. The women in the pictures are not considered human enough to worry about. An example of this syndrome was the response given by a Canada Customs official in the wake of women's protests against the distribution of the December 1984 edition of *Penthouse*. In that edition, a photographic feature showed women tightly bound and hanging motionless from trees and poles or splayed on rocks. The spread looked like a revelation of the necrophiliac pornographic mind, and a sign that dead women were sexually appealing. When asked to comment on how these materials escaped the scrutiny of otherwise over-vigilant border guards, a Customs representative hemmed and hawed and finally allowed that "the violence was implied."[3]

This incident shows that pornography's dynamic goes beyond the pictures, for although violence is clearly there on the screen or in the picture, viewers have difficulty seeing it as violence. Pornography distorts their perceptions. The case of Linda Marchiano is a reminder of another truth — that the women in pornography are real, that they live and breathe and hurt. She reminds us that when we see consent on the screen, there literally may be a lot more going on than meets the eye. These facts, plus the fact that pornography exists for something beyond the pictures and words — namely, sexual gratification — shows why it's necessary to take into account more than just the pictures and words in assessing pornography.

Feminism has always taken women's real experience as the basis for theory, and a perspective on pornography should not be any different. It is important to dispense with appearances and to reject any assumptions about what women are and what is real for us. Behind the facade of marital bliss, there could be wife assault. Similarly, behind the appearance of consent and pleasure in pornography, there could be rape and violation. To find out if there is, rigorous questions have to be asked, questions that probe women's actual experience and the way the products of pornography are used. *Pornography is a practice of sexual subordination. Its producers present sexual subordination for their own sexual pleasure, and its consumers get sexual pleasure from the presentation of sexual subordination.*

To understand pornography as a practice, it's necessary to dispense with the idea that pornography is a thing, a two-dimensional artifact, and consider it more a series of activities. Compare it to the practice of photography in which a photographer carries out a number of functions. S/he sets up the subject, focusses the lens, takes the picture, develops it and then sells it or exhibits it. Or compare it to the practice of advertising. The advertiser does market research, designs the ad, produces it, secures the ad space and displays it. The advertiser who practices advertising produces an advertisement. The photographer practicing photography produces a photograph. The pornographer practicing pornography produces...what? Resurrecting the word pornograph[4] makes the scheme consistent. The elements of presentation and sexual subordination are already contained in the word "pornography." Pornography comes from the Greek words *graphos*, meaning depiction, and *pornos*, the lowest of female sexual slaves. *Graphos* suggests that the activity of presentation is a crucial part of the process. Up until recently, depiction would have meant drawings or words or stage productions. In contemporary usage it can refer to the taking of pictures, or recording on video or audio tape as well. *Pornos* reminds us that the word was never used for playful or loving couplings but for the active subordination of the most degraded female slaves.

Having taken care to define the pornography, it is important not to abuse the term and so deprive it of its meaning. All things explicitly horrifying are not pornographic. People often use the word pornography to apply to violence and war, thus expressly avoiding the sexual component of the word. War is hell, but it is not necessarily pornographic. Violence is dreadful but it is not necessarily pornographic. Saying that it is obscures the particular way women are used in and affected by pornography.

A good way to understand how pornography is constructed as a practice is to examine child pornography. When an adult has sex with a child he is exercising sexual power over someone powerless; he is sexually subordinating that child. Many times he begins the process of subordination by showing his victim pornographs that introduce sexual ideas and teach the child how to behave sexually. Then he often takes her picture, either while having sex or afterwards. The picture is important to the victimizer because he tends to want a record of the sexual assault. In the picture, his victim will never grow old. By using the picture as a sexual stimulus, he can have sex with his victim forever. Pedophiles exchange child pornographs and even hook up with each other via computer.

This is how pornography works. A record of sexual abuse is shared so as to validate the sexual abuse that has occurred. Seen this way, it is hard to construe pornography as a safety valve or a phenomenon guaranteed to prevent the next sex crime. What point is there in saying, "If I did not have this picture as a sexual stimulus I would rape a real child," when a child was raped in order to make the picture in the first place? Bear in mind that during this process, not a penny need have been exchanged. In fact, many child pornographers keep their pornographs for themselves. Still, even without commercial distribution, these pictures are part of the pornographic process. Commercial distribution increases profits and provides a new motive for more sexual subordination, but the object of the pornographic exercise, whether produced by an industry or privately, is sex, not money.

While most would agree that having sex with a child subordinates her, having sex with an adult woman is, quite understandably, not seen in the same way. But the fact is that rarely will a person encounter sexually explicit materials featuring adults that are not records of sexual subordination. The abuses experienced by women in these products range from the pain of assault and torture acted out in violent pornography; to prior sexual assaults that distort women's perceptions of themselves and their choices and drive them into the pornography business where they get paid for what has previously been stolen from them — their bodies; to the coercion of poverty that limits women's job opportunities and makes the pornography business seem lucrative; to the subtler conditioning that teaches women that being a sex object — even in *Playboy* — is what every woman should dream of. Still, many people have a hard time looking at pornography and seeing victimization. Perhaps the best way to grasp the pain of these women is to put yourself into the picture and imagine how it would feel.

Of course a great deal of pornography does feature men with women, but the subordination factor does not work in the same way on men as it does on women. Stereotyping, as we will see, is a powerful force in pornography, but being stereotyped as dominant creates a different experience than being stereotyped as submissive. A male pornography performer interviewed in the film *Not a Love Story* made it clear that he didn't feel abused in the scenarios. As he eloquently put it, "It was very obvious that the camera revolved around the tip of my dick."

The definition of pornography provided here does not offer the means for us to know pornography when we see it. In violent pornography we should be able to see the subordination on its face. But often child pornographs are just pictures of children assaulted by pedophiles. Sometimes they are not sexually explicit and the children are fully clothed. In other cases where materials seem to have "just sex" written on them, we should never separate what we see from what we may not know. Who is the woman in the picture? How did she get there? What do we think of these conditions?

Defined as the presentation of sexual subordination for sexual pleasure, pornography is not presented here as a neutral term. Thus it differs from the term "sexually explicit materials," which is often used to define pornography and which makes it possible for pornography to go either way: it could be positive, it could be negative. Defining pornography as a practice of subordination embodies the harm, the negative, in the very definition. Subordination means that someone is being made less than someone else. It contains connotations of inequality and oppression. Where there is a presentation of sexual subordination for sexual pleasure, there is pornography. Where there is no sexual subordination in a presentation, there is no pornography. This means that some materials heretofore identified as pornography, by law or by moralists, would not be covered by the definition. For example, public displays of sexuality are not necessarily pornography. Neither are home-made videos of sexual activity. Crucially, with this definition, the only way to be "pro-pornography" is to take a stand in favour of sexual subordination.

What is subordinating? What is not? This definition does leave room for some personal judgements and tends to vex those who would prefer a right/wrong approach to the matter, echoing a masculinist aversion to ambiguity.[5] But these things *are* complex. For instance, consider the Venus de Milo. One person might be concerned that calling it pornographic trivializes the real harm pornography does to women. That person believes presentations of female nudes are not per se subordinating. But another, wishing to convey the pervasiveness of sexual subordination, even in art, might say such presentations *are* subordinating. Someone else may add that presentations of nude women are not subordinating if there as many presentations of male nudes on the same page. Another person might consider that view mere liberal folly, and insist that equality on one page does not undo the inequality that pervades the products of our culture everywhere else. Still another person using the insights of feminist film theory might contend that the element of subordination is there in the very taking of the picture.

What follows is one view of what sexual subordination is and when it is part of the practice of pornography. Some of this perspective is influenced by the four elements Andrea Dworkin has identified as the distinct features of subordination: hierarchy, objectification, the dynamic of dominance and submission, and violence.[6] I won't cover these four elements separately, but instead will weave them into the discussion of sexual subordination as it unfolds. We will discover that subordination is sexual when it is acted out in the feelings and dynamics of sex itself, so that in sex men emerge powerful and women wind up powerless. This is how sex is gendered — a term aptly describes how certain social phenomena are constructed along sex lines.

Sexual subordination occurs in a number of different ways.

One example of sexual subordination occurs when explicitly violent pornographs present women being hurt — killed, tortured or beaten. When I refer to violence in pornography in this instance, I am not referring to mainstream pin-ups caressed by leather (although as we shall see, these too have subordinating qualities), but to explicitly violent scenarios like those in *Water Power*, or home-made bondage films in which the violence is not staged. In these scenarios, objectification is obviously taking place. Objectification is the process through which the person on the bottom of the hierarchy is dehumanized, made less human than the person on the top of the hierarchy, who in turn becomes the standard for what human is. In violent pornography, objectification takes place so effectively that many people can look at these pictures and not see anyone getting hurt.

Sexual subordination also occurs anytime a woman is forced into a sexual act for its presentation. This is Linda Marchiano's experience and the experience of many women who have been forced to perform sexually for a camera. For example, in one Ontario shelter, a woman confided to a counsellor that her husband had tied her to the bed, forced her into sexual acts with the family dog and then took her picture. When this kind of subordination takes place, it is often very difficult to identify from the picture itself, since often the women are depicted as getting pleasure from the sexual abuse even in explicitly sexually subordinating scenes.

One of the favourite fictions of pornography is that women play an acquiescent role in their own degradation. Pornographers espouse this egregious lie when they depict women enjoying rape. In clinical circles where the effects of these scenes on viewer attitudes have been studied, researchers call these scenes rape myths.[7] The promulgation of the rape myth is an important pornographic strategy, for it provides the means for disguising whatever force may have been used in the making of the pornographs. What looks like rape suddenly becomes sex when the victim moans with delight. We are already reluctant to see violation in the pictures that show explicit violence, and the sight of a woman apparently getting pleasure from torture skews our perceptions even more. We see a woman raped, but wait, she's enjoying it. Maybe it isn't rape at all. We don't see what is going on off camera, who else is there, or how she got there in the first place.

Even as technological advance has defined contemporary culture, many movie lovers become unsettled when they see a film and then see footage of how the film was made. We don't want to see the lighting crew, the heavy equipment, the painted set, the truck, the stunt men, the make-up crew and the director telling the actors exactly how to read the lines against the blazing sunset. We want the fantasy intact. We agree to suspend disbelief when pornography replaces the blazing sunset on the screen. Movie myths obscure the coercion that goes into the making of pornographs. So it is not surprising that while watching pornographs of women being brutalized, some people forget that there is real pain there.

The myths of pornography have become more credible than the voice of real women. Faced with a film in which she performs fellatio with apparent eagerness, people do not believe Linda Marchiano when she says it was an act, that she didn't like it, that she was forced to do it. Marchiano's performance was real, and not simulated. She did "deep throat" Harry Reems, her co-performer, just as women really do get hurt in violent pornography. This is why I do not use words like "simulated" when referring to the action in specific pornographs. There is, after all, no such thing as a simulated vagina. I do not think there is any such thing, for that matter, as simulated sex. Just because there is no penetration does not mean that the women in the pictures are not real. Similarly, I avoid other words that have been associated with the discourse on pornography, like "images" and "representation." These are words that have an important meaning in art criticism, but they tend to distance us from what is happening to the women in pornographic pictures. Instead of the word image, I use "document." Thus, pornographs are not images of sex, they are documents of sexual events. And pornography is a presentation of sexual subordination. It does not represent anyone or anything.

A woman has been sexually subordinated when pictures of her are used or sold without her consent. This can happen when a woman discovers that her husband has sent in photographs of her as part of the reader participation feature in pornographic magazines. It happened to former Miss America Vanessa Williams and to pop star Madonna, who early in their careers had both posed in the nude for photographers. *Penthouse* publisher Bob Guccione was able to let legal loopholes and rubber-stamp releases pass as consent and then published pictures of these women when they became public figures. He made immense profits without financially compensating the two women. In *Screw* Al Goldstein presented a drawing of Gloria Steinem's face on a body that had an explicit rendering of genitalia. These public displays of major figures are meant to be humiliating, and the damage can and has been devastating.[8]

When a woman in a pornograph is owned by a pornographer, when she is his possession, then she is being sexually subordinated. This applies to the Hugh Hefner syndrome in which bunnies, many of whom have had sex with Hefner, are paraded on the page as a graphic depiction of the pornographer's virility. It also applies to husbands who take pictures of their wives in the bedroom to show proof of ownership. And it applies to women who sell themselves so that pornography can be made. In fact, the industry's ability to churn out commercially available pornography depends on the traffic in real women.

When people look at women in pornography, they often do not see victims subordinated in the practice. They see pornography's collaborators: Why do these women do it?, they ask. If they stopped, wouldn't the industry collapse immediately? These questions are part of a syndrome called blaming the victim. Victim-blamers who look at pornography wonder why the women are there rather than why there is such an enormous market for sexually abusive entertainment. The fact is that the women in pornography are usually women trapped in systems of prostitution. Either they lack the skills to do anything else or, as we will see in the last chapter, selling their bodies has become a logical extension of other sexual abuses in their lives.

Many prostitutes prefer the work in pornography to other ways of dealing in sex. For one thing, the pornography business is marginally safer. It is true that women have found themselves vulnerable in violent pornographic scenarios, but in other kinds of pornography, they are less vulnerable than they might be in a car or alley where no one can see what the johns are doing to them. As well, women in pornography usually have sex with fewer clients than women working the streets all day, and sometimes they perform sexually with men they know instead of a constant stream of strangers. This means that anti-pornography activists have to be aware of how their activities may affect the lives of working prostitutes.

Occasionally, there is slightly more money in the pornography industry than in prostitution. Street prostitutes can be photographed in short sessions for more money than they would make turning a trick, and high-income prostitutes can make even more money in the booming business of pornographic film. But pornography still takes place within a deeply oppressive system in which women's choices are either dictated or circumscribed.

As it is, women do not make all that much money from their work in the pornography industry. Playboy "playmates," whose salaries are often cited as proof of women's collaboration in pornography, may get as much as as $10,000 for their feature spread (as well as the privilege of sleeping with Hefner). But there are only 12 playmates a year, hardly enough to provide opportunities for the thousands of women in the sex industry, and certainly not enough to indicate that the industry is lucrative for women. In a business that has made millionaires out of pornographic video producers, none of the highest paid so-called stars has ever made a six-figure annual income, and most of the salaries of sexually explicit performers hover in the $50,000 range. It is only the illusion of lucre that keeps women in the business, burdening them with the false hope that they can make it, that it's only a matter of time. In the meantime, women actually make between $50 for small quickie operations to $500 a day for photographs in the established mainstream trade, but rarely will an established photographer use a model more than once a year. In one typical California studio, only three models worked twice the same year.[9]

An exchange of money between buyer and seller tends to be viewed as an automatic sign of consent. This is simply strong testimony to the power of the dollar, and it ignores the circumstances that drive women to "consent" to being photographed nude for a paltry $50. So potent is the dollar that it is also perceived as having the miraculous power to negate whatever right to abuse has been bought. If a woman, for whatever reasons — poverty, an inability to control her life circumstances — sells someone the right to beat her up and the attack takes place, she *has* been assaulted. She *has* been hurt. The bruises do not disappear just because she has some cash in her fist. And she is not a collaborator, she is a survivor trying to get on with her life. Pornographers depend on this kind of desperation, for if women had more choice in life, more control over their own bodies and who gets access to them, pornographers would have no one to subordinate for the pleasure of their consumers.

2

PORNOGRAPHY IS BIG BUSINESS. But the definition of pornography used here does not depend on the commercial distribution of the pornographs, because the practice can exist without the exchange of money. The facts about child pornography, especially the fact that pedophiles are more likely to exchange pornographs than to sell them, tell us that pornography can exist without a well-oiled business machine. Adult pornographers also often hang on to their home-made pornographs rather than put them on the market. Besides, pornography does exist in non-capitalist countries where sexual subordination has maintained its appeal even though there are few free enterprisers to market it. The commoditization of sexuality and the hunger for profits promote pornography but do not define it.

On the other hand, there is no question that big business has made sexual subordination viable and more visible to more people than ever before. Traffickers have a knack for exploiting new technologies. Set up a system of communications and the pornographers soon show up. Pay television licensees in Canada did not have their licenses for three months before "adult" programming began to appear on the schedules. Now that hotel rooms can be wired up for pornography, there are more than 15,000 hotel rooms in Toronto alone in which customers can participate in the practice of pornography by dialing the phone or pressing the remote buttons on their TVs.

During Canada's deepest recession in 1982, Red Hot Video, taking advantage of the home video boom, defied every economic trend and opened fifteen outlets in British Columbia in the space of three months. Red Hot Video and its competitor Ultra Blue Video rent the products of pornography produced in the United States. Customers can order them by phone and pay by credit card. Vancouver millionaire Jim Pattison, chairman of the board of Expo 86, controls Mainland Magazines, which distributes close to 250 "men's sophisticates." Rogers Cable in Toronto controls Transworld Communications, which is the company that serves up pornographs in hotel rooms. Pornography is practiced by some of Canada's most respectable businesses.

It is the sheer volume that counts when it comes to assessing the impact of the product. Because pornographs are produced in such huge quantities, pornographers can stereotype men and women very effectively. Literally, stereotype means a process through which copies made from a second-generation version are repeated in a fixed and unchanging form. The word stereotype is entirely appropriate in a pornographic context. Most commercial pornographs present a second-generation version of women and men — the pornographers' version. Stereotyping is by its nature systematic, and in the case of pornography, subordinating for women.

To appreciate fully how stereotyping works, pornographs should be seen in large numbers. As a group, they all tend to look the same. This fact challenges the wishful and sometimes willful thinking of observers who claim that pornography reveals an astonishing range of sexual possibilities. It's difficult to see any such range when pornography presents women many times more often than men; pornographs, on their face, don't even manage to take into account both genders, let alone the presumed range of sexual practices. If pornographers were as imaginative about sexuality as they are about how they can subordinate in new and different ways, the discussion might be quite different.

As it is, pornography does not present men nearly as often as women. This is mainly because male consumers have little interest in purchasing access to men's bodies, although they do appreciate watching men subordinate women. An important factor in limiting the presence of men in pornography is Canadian law. Canada's obscenity law makes it illegal to distribute materials that unduly exploit sex, sex and violence, sex and cruelty, sex and horror, etc. The litany of cases on the jurisprudential record indicates that sex has been defined by the presence of an erect penis or penetration of body orifices by penises or objects. What this means is that a presentation of a woman nude, gagged, bound, nipples clipped, is not obscene. There is no "sex" there.

According to the law, the penis is so sacred, scary or profane, it must be hidden at all costs. The costs wind up being paid by women whose vulvae and breasts can be displayed in explicit detail without a single legal sanction. The law may say that the penis equals sex, but the effect of the law is to create an array of cultural products which give the distinct impression that sex equals women and women only. And the huge volume of these materials makes the corollary seem true: women equal sex and sex only.

Women in pornography are sexual in particular ways. Examples of the rape myth are legion, but a film entitled *All the King's Ladies* offers a particularly clear example. In it a woman is taken and forced into a field where she is raped with a whip handle by a man masked as an executioner. The victim struggles at first but then she submits with pleasure. The scenario makes it appear that she does not know herself sexually, that "no" means "yes," or that "no" can become "yes" with some heavy pressure. After the assault, she expresses her appreciation by licking the weapon that was used to violate her.

Pornographers give the impression that women are insatiable, never able to get enough sex. This is obvious in films like *Inside Seka*, in which the title character displays sexual voracity with three partners, without any plot cluttering things up. This female insatiability is featured as well in the December 1983 edition of *OUI* magazine, which featured a photographic spread entitled "Crawling from the Wreckage." In the series, a woman is photographed draped over and inside a car that has just been demolished in an accident. She is covered in blood, and her clothes are torn away, laying her breasts and vagina bare as she stares into the camera with a come-on pout. Even crawling from the wreckage, she is ready for sex.

When women do not behave like sexual hysterics, they are ridiculed and punished. In a pornographic takeoff of *Raiders of the Lost Ark*, a woman is taken prisoner by a villainess who ties her up and forces her to watch her slaves have sex in what looks like a prelude to the prisoner's own rape. The hero arrives just as the prisoner is about to be attacked. He ignores the ingenue and takes up with the villainess instead, leaving the prisoner bound and humiliated as punishment for her failure to conform to pornographic convention: she did not automatically join in sex at the sight of it or eagerly anticipate being sexually assaulted. Her terror is trivialized as prudishness worthy of ridicule. In the pornographic universe women have no fear of great sex, and great sex includes rape. This is how the pornographer serves up his second-generation version — his stereotype — of women and what they are.

Women are depicted in pornography as commodities to be bought and sold, as so sexually submissive that they fall happily into the role of sexual servant. In a science fiction pornograph called *The Satiators of Alpha Blue*, the pornographic vision sees men and women totally segregated. Men do the real work, while women do the sexual work in a vast brothel. After work, the men are able to dial-a-whore and the women are happily compliant, consigned to a life of blissful sexual slavery. One man and one woman, however, express dissident views and look for love in a loveless and sex-drunk world. In the end, they live happily ever after.

In the past, this kind of plot device granted to the work what has become known as "redeeming social value." The presence of redeeming social value — often apparent on the last page of a book where mutual love takes over from the sexual subordination of everything that came before, or the last scene of a film in which the sexual adventurers reform and marry — greatly reduced the chances of pornographic works being found obscene in American courts.[10] The "love story" plot of *The Satiators of Alpha Blue* is a flimsy device for the depiction of a fantasy of sexual class control of men over women, and of a sexual practice in which women are out of their minds with desire while men reap the sexual benefits.

Note that in *Inside Seka*, the *Raiders* takeoff and *Satiators*, there is no violence, no rape, no paraphernalia, no whips, no chains. Apart from the vague suggestion that women, along with the semen spilled on top of them, can be discarded after use, the materials reveal consenting adults who are sexually active. Still, there is an eerie inevitablity to the narratives. Men maintain sexual control with a steely rod while women are on the way to going sexually berserk. Women spread their legs for anyone and anything — men most of the time, objects and animals occasionally. The Satiators were delighted to be called up by anyone who had the money. Even the lovers who couple ecstatically in the end do so true to pornographic form — he in total control, she over the edge, he being aroused by her failure to control herself, she aroused by his ability to control her.

This is the way pornography fuses male sexual practice with dominance and female sexual practice with submission. In the explicitly brutal pornographs, male sexuality looks like that of a rapist and female sexuality looks like that of a rape victim, until she comes, at which point female sexuality looks like submission after some heavy persuasion. In the world of pornography, men take women, hurt women, fuck them and use them, while women are hurt, fucked, used and enjoy it. This is pornography's perfect congruent universe.[11]

It remains so even when pornographers present their versions of lesbianism to their male readers. In those scenarios, the male reader has not one but two women to whom he can have sexual access, two women he can metaphorically fuck, use and enjoy. In video scenarios, this dynamic of dominance becomes obvious when one or two men interrupt the two women and give them "what they really need." As for the lesbian spreads in heterosexually-oriented magazines, contrary to the views of some lesbians who defend lesbian content no matter who presents it and who profits from it, the scenarios shown in this kind of pornography are not validations for a lesbian identity or for sexual diversity. They are there to fit neatly into the stereotype of the hopelessly lascivious woman: women are so horny, so desperate for sex, so willing to spread their legs, that they will even do it for other women.

The pornographic universe also remains intact in the pornography lesbians and gay men produce for their own communities. The women and men who "perform" are in pornography because they are poor, have been recruited into pornography in the course of a sexual assault, or, having fallen into the victimization syndrome, are being revictimized. Not only are the experiences of these pornography "stars" like those of the women victimized in straight pornography sold to men, but the ideologies embedded in gay materials also usually mimic the messages in heterosexual pornography. The ideology of dominance and submission is deeply entrenched in the overtly sadomasochistic material in lesbian magazines like *On Our Backs*. The fact that the ideology of dominance and submission can transcend heterosexuality speaks to the power of gender stereotypes. In gay male pornographic scenarios of dominance and submission, the person doing the fucking is often called "he," while the fuckee is called "she." This is the way gay pornography, even though it is same-sex material, still manages to gender sexuality. The sexes are the same but the roles remain different — masculine and feminine, powerful and powerless.

In the pornographic universe, racism is very sexually appealing. When pornographers use black women, they place them in scenarios of slavery that fuse male dominance with racial superiority. In her chains, the black pornographic female looks as if she enjoys being enslaved in both the racial and sexual senses. The pornography of Asian women is often a pornography of torture and ultra-passivity, perpetuating white western stereotypes of Asian women as passive and subservient. Some people have suggested that any stereotype of race constitutes the pornography of race,[12] but they miss the fundamental point that the sexual component cannot be removed from a definition of pornography. Racism per se is not pornographic. Rather, pornography eroticizes racism. And one of this society's most successful strategies for instituting values is to eroticize them.

Although many people do not want to pin the pornography label on the likes of *Penthouse* and *Playboy*, they do fit the definition of pornography used here. Sexual subordination goes on in mainstream pornography when women's powerlessness is reinforced by their consistent infantilization. Florence Rush contends that the a woman-child is fast becoming the sexual ideal.[13] They are not, after all, called playmates for nothing. The centrefold or pin-up plays an important part in the process described by Rush. The centrefold is always young and nubile, her image purposely altered to make her so. Youth not only conveys beauty by the standards of the west, it conveys an absence of power,[14] a sexuality that is entirely unthreatening, one which the user can shape, tutor and then conquer. Even body hair, the indication of maturity in women, disappears so that the pin-up can look young and vulnerable (except, of course, for pubic hair, although it too is shaved in some pornographs for readers who find that appealing).

This powerlessness is emphasized when mainstream pornographers sexually subordinate women by turning them into objects. *Playboy* crams photos of women between photos of good Scotch and fine cars, making it appear as if the women too are commodities and easily bought. The putatively harmless centrefold makes women appear to be naturally exhibitionist, empty vessels to be taken by the reader. The women sometimes do not have last names, since last names would bestow upon them something that approximates a real identity. Instead we discover Mandy, Amber, Candy and other confections that form a never-ending line of hypersexualized clones. Once in a while the pin-up is graced with an astrological sign, but for the most part she is nobody except for her sex, and good for little else.

This mainstream female sexual ideal is not as directly promiscuous as the sexual hysteric of explicit videos, but she is lascivious in a more insidious way. The mainstream pin-up opens her legs to reveal a big zero that is only something when it is filled. The pin-up is shown as even less choosy than her explicit counterpart since she is available to anyone who purchases the magazine. The dynamic between pin-up and consumers is that of a gang bang. *Penthouse* publisher Bob Guccione rationalizes his business by insisting that women are natural exhibitionists and men are natural voyeurs. He likes to feature women alone in some kind of private activity so that the reader will get the feeling he's spying. The camera literally captures the woman for the male gaze. In other magazines, the pin-up stares into the camera with a head-on gaze, something consumers apparently like a lot. But whether her privacy is invaded or whether her eye invites the reader to fill the hole between her legs, she is always acted upon. She is a static object there to be invaded.

In North America, a photo of a woman primed for sexual intercourse, her legs spread, her labia wet — cheesecake is the term some people use to describe this undraped female form — is distributed en masse all over the continent. A photo of a man with an erection, however, is obscene according to Canadian law, and according to American mores, not the kind of thing a distributor can put on the newsstand next to *Time* and *Newsweek*. It is in fact extremely difficult to turn men into sexual objects for display. Consider Bob Guccione's experiment with *Viva* magazine. The idea of *Viva* was to sell beefcake to women the way *Penthouse* sold cheesecake to men. *Viva*, first published in 1972, featured explicit prose accounts of women's sexual adventures punctuated with photos of nude men, their penises not erect.

Where to put the magazine on the newsstand? Alongside *Playboy* and *Penthouse*, it would not find its targeted audience. Alongside *Chatelaine* and *Good Housekeeping*, it might cause apoplexy among the readers of those fairly staid magazines. Eventually, thanks to Guccione's marketing skills, *Viva* did find its audience. But the novelty wore off and gradually, female readers began to complain that the men in *Viva* looked gay. They did not look the way *Viva*'s readers wanted sexy men to look.

Viva's editors had done everything they could to convey the virility of the men in the magazine. They knew, having done it in *Penthouse*, that if you spread a woman's legs and placed her in front of the camera with a head-on gaze, she will convey sex. They suspected that if male models were manipulated in the same way, they might not convey sex so easily. So they placed the men in forest settings, staring out into the distance to make it appear that they had control over the space around them. Sometimes they were posed on horseback to affect the Marlboro look. But it didn't work. These men, readers said, looked like homosexuals. *Viva*, which eventually foundered and disappeared, was an important experiment in objectification: reduce a woman to tits and ass and she looks like a woman. Reduce a man to pecs and ass and he looks by conventional standards less than a real man.

Pornographers like to describe themselves as the bearers of dissident ideas. But women are not ideas, and pimping women to readers is not an expression of political dissent. The numbers speak most eloquently. The notion that pornographers are struggling against a repressive status quo is difficult to take seriously in the face of industry profits greater than those of the conventional film and record industries combined.

3

FAR FROM EXPRESSING DISSENT, pornography's message is becoming the cultural norm. Sexually subordinating values expressed in the practice of pornography are present everywhere else in mass culture. People have been complaining for years that advertisers use sex to sell commodities. More accurately, advertisers exploit women, who equal sex, to sell commodities. When they do this, they are not advertising just the product, they are advertising the sexual value of exploitation. When an advertisement for jackets by Sergio Valente shows a man about to assault a woman, making it look like sex so that the jacket looks more appealing, the ad not only promotes the jacket, it also promotes that particular kind of sex. The stereotypes of sex Sergio Valente and other advertisers sell are the same ones pornographers perpetuate. Pornographers tell us women are easy to get. So do advertisers when they insinuate that all you have to do to get the woman sprawled on a car is buy the car.

The new cultural force of rock video already appears to be conforming to pornographic standards. Rick James' rape video of the song "Give It To Me" features the singer storming into his house demanding sex from his girlfriend. He refuses to take no for an answer and he submits her to sexual force that she appears to enjoy. The video was produced in 1981, the dawn of the rock video age, but things have not really changed much. Michael Jackson's 1988 video of "The Way You Make Me Feel" features Jackson and a gang stalking a woman in a scenario that is disturbingly misogynist.

Many rock videos use the pornographic conventions of sexual subordination. No wonder the Playboy Channel packaged and broadcasts the most explicit rock videos under the program title *Hot Rocks*. In the now classic video "Girls on Film" by Duran Duran, produced in 1983, the ratio of women to men is 10 to 1. With the exception of the band members, who remain arty and aloof, all of the participants in the video are involved in sexual play. The nude women, mud wrestling or slithering along poles or fighting with pillows that tear and release a mountain of feathers (chick imagery, perhaps), look as if they have just stepped off the set of an x-rated film.

As "Girls on Film" proceeds, a waterlogged woman, water dripping from her mouth, is given mouth-to-mouth resuscitation by a man at the side of a swimming pool. Within seconds, she surprises him by sticking her tongue in his mouth, whereupon the two begin to roll around on the patio. The scenario is reminiscent of *OUI*'s "Crawling from the Wreckage," in which even after a hideous car accident, the woman wants sex. Of course, women know how unlikely it is that sex would be on a woman's mind after she extricates herself from a crumpled car. Anyone who has swallowed a load of lakewater, let alone come close to drowning, knows how unlikely it is that the woman in "Girls on Film" would want sex the moment she recovered her first breath. But this video is committed to the promotion of the stereotype that women are primed for sex at all times.

Pornography merges with mass culture, but it merges with high culture as well. A painting by Jules Garnier (1873) features a nude sprawled out on the rocks of a tropical island. She is being eyed by two islanders who have found her. The painting is entitled *The Shipwreck Victim*, but one would never know that this woman had just been tossed up from the sea. She lounges on robes that have appeared there conveniently, her eye is cast toward the spectator as she reclines in full frontal nudity. Except for the absence of blood, the narrative is almost a replica of "Crawling from the Wreckage." She is plainly a sexual find.[15] In making it appear that a woman could be ready for sex, Garnier constructs women the way pornographers do, telling us that women are ready for sex, no matter what the circumstances. "Girls on Film" showed that pornographic values have become the cultural norm. Garnier's painting indicates that pornographic values have been the cultural ideal for hundreds of years.

This kind of analysis worries art-lovers, who are certain that if the feminist critique of pornography maintains its intensity, and investigates too closely the meaning, form and process of artistic production, the nudes of the art world will also become suspect. They are actually quite right. For, like the pornography star, the nudes in the masterpieces of the art world are real women with real experience. One ought to ask the same questions about them as one does about the women in pornography. Who are they? How did they get into the pictures? The subjects of Boucher's nudes, for instance, were usually members of King Louis XV's stable of mistresses. King Louis did not exhibit his paintings publicly just to prove his association with one of the great artists of the day. He exhibited them as a means of boasting of his sexual prowess. To be painted was to be owned. To be exhibited was to be advertised. Goya caused a sensation when he unveiled *The Naked Maya* because he was revealing more than a painting. He was disclosing a secret affair with the subject.

Is there really much difference between the consumer of *Playboy* musing on the sexual satiation of Hugh Hefner and the contemporaries of King Louis or Goya admiring their virility? King Louis' mistresses were by definition sexually subordinated, royalty being disinclined to take no for an answer. Many other subjects for the "ideal" form were similarly subjected. Boucher's paintings were usually hung in the king's apartments after their initial public showing, there to lend sexual ambience and to be viewed in the course of the king's sexual relations. All of these conditions make these high art monuments pornographs and part of the practice of pornography.

We lose track of the pervasiveness of the pornographic dynamic when we locate it only among the lower classes, calling their practice pornography and excusing the upper classes for their interest in erotica. The only difference between low-class pornography and high-class erotica are the production values and the number of syllables in the words. Sanitizing the high-class materials by calling them erotica does not erase their pornographic impulse, for virtuosity of expression does not make a presentation any less pornographic. The Marquis de Sade routinely kidnapped, raped and tortured girls.[16] The elegance of the language he used to describe these things does not change the nature of the acts. He committed these crimes and people who read about them find them sexually arousing. The Marquis knew that they would. He is not a dissident, though he is often revered as such, and he is not worthy of respect, though his works grace the shelves of the most respectable readers. He is a pornographer.

If art can turn the values of sexual subordination into the ideal, fashion magazines turn them into an exercise in sophistication. New-wave fashion has stepped up the sadomasochistic imagery, suggesting the new *haut* sexuality of dominance and submission. Even without the aesthetic of menace, the fashion model is often presented in the same pose as the pin-up. In fact, fashion magazines do to the female face what pornographers do to the female body: turn it into something sexual. Just as pornographers highlight women's sexual parts, their genitalia and their breasts, fashion photographers emphasize the mouth, that part of the face that can kiss or suck. The pin-up's face is dry except for the mouth and eyes, which are made to look wet and seductive. The mouth pouts and the eyes are blackened to connote a bruised sexuality.[17] It is almost impossible to view a woman staring out of a fashion magazine cover without interpreting her gaze as sexual. (If a man were staring out as vacantly, he could just as easily be interpreted as wondering who won the ballgame). In one of Toronto's remaining sex shops, *Vogue* is displayed alongside *Hustler* and *Penthouse*.

By saying that mass culture testifies to the mainstreaming of pornographic values, I am not saying that pornography is the same as the products of mass culture, or that the influence of the products of mass culture is as pernicious as the products of pornography. Some cultural critics do think so, however, arguing that an ad for Wisk, which ridicules women who haven't been able to remove ring-around-the-collar, or an ad for floor wax, which make it seem as if women's self-esteem hinges on whether their floors shine, subordinate women as much as any pornographic product. But there is surely a difference between an ad for Wisk and a violent pornograph. The difference begins in the conditions under which these products are produced. No doubt, the casting couch is a fixture everywhere in the entertainment business, and many models in the fashion industry or in TV advertisements have had to put up with sexual pressure in order to land a job. But in the production phase of pornography there is rape and assault. The difference between the sexual harassment in the entertainment industry and the rape in pornography is a matter of degree, but I think the degree matters.

More important, in mass media sexual stereotypes are often presented for entertainment, but the sexual harassment that went into the making of the product is not presented as the entertainment itself. It is the sexual abuse itself that is the turn-on in pornography. Both the pornograph and the Wisk ad are advertisements, one for a detergent, one for sexual subordination. Both are ads for sexual inequality. But only the pornograph eroticizes inequality, presenting sexual subordination specifically for sexual pleasure.

4

JUST AS AN ADVERTISER cannot keep a client unless his ad strategy sells the product, so the pornographer will lose his customers if his product doesn't "work." Users know their pornographers and who makes the best stuff. "Best" in this case means the most arousing. Pornographers know this. They know what to make, and the distributors know what to sell.[18] It is thus not only what the customer *sees* that matters but how what he sees makes him *feel* that keeps the industry going. The better the orgasm, the better the pornograph. The dynamic of pornography does not stop with the stereotypes in the pictures, or even the sexual subordination presented there, but rather with what these pictures do for consumers.

It does seem almost unbelievable that billions of dollars are invested in sexual subordination on this continent so that consumers, usually men, can come. No wonder there has been resistance, even in feminist quarters, to accepting the enormity of the situation. The resistance was articulated in the first stages of the feminist protest against pornography, when activists insisted that it was the violence that bothered women, not the sex, forgetting that the purpose for all this unspeakable violence was to give a man an erection. The resistance persisted with the generous interpretation of pornographs as "images," "signifiers" or "fantasy,"[19] anything to avoid having to cope with the truth — that there are real women in the pictures and that an erection, any way you look at it, is not a fantasy.

Some, perhaps wanting to reinforce the belief that men can be rehabilitated or can change (a belief I would like to share), insist that all this sexual subordination is an expression of male fear of women, or an expression of shame, or an expression of men's frustration in a mean and brutal world in which they themselves are hopelessly oppressed. This may be true. It is also true that pornographers can and do exploit men and their fears. But the central dynamic of pornography itself has been misconstrued in this analysis.

Men use pornography primarily because it feels good. What feels good is male domination and female submission. What feels good is watching women in conditions of subordination. What feels good is the apparently unlimited and protected access men have to female sexuality in the form of commercially available pornographs. What feels good is the existence of a population of women for *them*. Many consumers, and even non-consumers, believe that this population of women materializes naturally to service men's sexual needs. Some women, they think, are "like that." The fact that these women appear in postures of humiliation and abuse in pornography only proves the point, and becomes a self-fulfilling prophecy for men who look at the pictures and decide that the women in them must be less than human or they would not do these things. The unobstructed access to female sexuality, coupled with definition of female sexuality as "less than" that of men, reinforces male power and turns women into a group that cannot be perceived as equal.

We've already seen how the advertiser wants the consumer to buy his product, while the pornographer wants the consumer to become sexually aroused. But the parallels between the advertiser and the pornographer go beyond the fact that both ply their trade in the hopes that their consumers will feel something: both rely on some form of imitation on the part of the user. The advertiser displays someone buying a product and getting pleasure from it in the hopes that the viewer, seeing this, will go out and buy the product. Often pornographers work in the same way, hoping the consumer will find a way to have the kind of sex the pornographs advertise.

Looking at the ads in bondage magazines, it becomes clear why it is so hard to separate the pornographs from actual sexual practice. Magazines specializing in sadomasochism contain ads for the paraphernalia required to get the sex promoted in the text. Often the pornographer, like Larry Flynt of *Hustler* magazine, owns the sex toy companies that advertise in his magazine. In other words, he has a specific financial interest in making sure the customer replicates the sexual acts in the magazine. So it should not be all that surprising that many consumers want to experience with live women the sexual subordination they find so arousing in the pornography.

Many women are not in situations where they can choose whether to participate with men in the sex promoted by the magazines. Women who have escaped to shelters for assaulted women have described how their spouses, inspired by pornography, have forced them to participate in sex they did not want.[20] When Diana Russell asked a random sample of women, "Have you ever been upset by someone trying to get you to do what they'd seen in pornographic movies or books?", 10 per cent of her respondents said yes.[21] We do not know how many of her sample were forced into sexual acts that they could not know were connected to pornographic materials.

This coercive sexual dynamic can be explained in part by pornography's promotion of the idea that "no" means "yes." It is an effective campaign. But another factor contributing to the rise in consumers' expectations of what women want and what women do is that so much of the sexual subordination that goes into the making of the pornograph is invisible to the user. The widespread objectification of women of course plays a part here; but above and beyond it there's the influence of pornographers who make the contorted positions of women in pornography seem easy and natural. One model went so far as to say that she knew she had the pose right when it started to hurt.[22] But the woman's ecstatic facial expression belies the effort necessary to create the pose. A sequence in the National Film Board's documentary *Not a Love Story* shows a woman posing for a mainstream magazine in a difficult position. Holding her leg up to her chin, she grows impatient and says, "Take the picture already," as she struggles to maintain the pose. But the consumer will see only the fiction of the model's grin. Her smile will convince him that anything is possible in the sexual arena and he may wonder why his own partner is not so nimble.

Russell's study provided some of the first evidence that the sexual subordination in the practice of pornography goes on not only during the process of production but during the process of consumption. And the evidence is growing. Many women report being forced to buy videos and watch them. They describe being bullied by partners who wonder why they don't look and act like the women in the pictures.[23] Now that the video boom has brought such a huge volume of new pornographs into the home, where most of the violence against women takes place, these conditions of force are worsening.

It is difficult to accept pornography's so-called cathartic value when murder victims' bodies are strewn with pornographs, or when the dresser drawers of child-killers like Clifford Olson are crammed with pornographic magazines. And from the point of view of those who have had pornography used against them, pornography looks more like a manual designed to teach abuse rather than a safety valve designed to prevent it. One American court felt strongly enough about the connection between pornography and violence that it agreed to hear a woman's suit against *Hustler* magazine. Her son had died of autoerotic asphyxia, strangling himself while masturbating and using ropes to cut off the oxygen to his brain. According to *Hustler*, which provided a detailed description of the technique in the edition lying at the feet of the dead boy, this greatly intensified orgasm.[24]

Proponents of the safety valve theory assume that pornography provides an outlet for oversexed men who would harass women if there weren't pornography available. If this were true, then over the last fifteen years, during which the pornography industry has increased its size 1,600 times over, sexual abuse ought to have almost disappeared. It has not. Taken together, over 90 per cent of American women will experience some kind of sexual abuse in their lifetime.[25] The figure for males is infinitesimal by comparison. This is why many feminists view violence against women as an issue of equality. The trauma of sexual violence sabotages women's mobility, their confidence and their belief that they can be effective in the world, while men make their way in the world without fear of attack.

Still, the relationship between the pornographs and assault is difficult to identify as causal. Even defining pornography as a practice, saying that it is made through sexual subordination, is not the same as saying that the pornographs cause the subordination or sexual abuse.[26] But then again, it is as hard to isolate the harm of pornographs in a sexist society as it is to isolate tobacco as a cause of cancer in a society that spews out all kinds of carcinogens as a matter of course. Most researchers, like Murray Straus, have had to settle for correlational data. Straus measured the readership of so-called men's magazines against the rape rate on a state-by-state basis. He found that Alaska and Nevada were number one and two respectively in both, and that the 10 states with the highest rape rate matched the states with the highest consumptions of the magazines.[27]

But even without this kind of data, if we believe what women say about their own lives — admittedly a radical research methodology — the case for the connection between pornographs and violent acts is strong enough. Saying so does not make the assailants less responsible for what they do. Identifying the dynamic of pornography, however, does place some responsibility on pornographers for promoting this kind of assault. Pornographers do not trade in fantasy. They trade in the sexual subordination they hope will sustain their customers' erections. What, we should ask, is supposed to happen to these erections? If we take what women say seriously, it is obvious that men do not confine their sexual activity in pornography to masturbation.

Feminists have found that violence against women is systematic and that pornographers have turned that violence into an erotic spectacle. It is painful to have to face the fact that terrible things are done to women to create this spectacle, and that the documents of this abuse, the pornographs themselves, are displayed and sold publicly with the assumption that not much will be done about the abuses shown. It has a devastating effect on women's sense of personal security, for all of this reinforces the suspicion (and the experience) that if these things were to happen to women outside of the practice of pornography, not a great deal would be done about it either. When a woman confronts the products of pornography she feels as if she is being targetted for abuse. In this way pornography acts as a form of public terrorism for women.

Big business means high visibility. While the potential for profit may lure pornographers into the industry, what matters to women as a group is the volume of pornographs available and visible. The constant reiteration of sexual stereotypes in pornography or its mass culture imitators makes the messages all the more persuasive and the impact all the more intense. The fact that recent studies indicate that the majority of pornography users are boys between the ages of 12 and 17 suggests that pornography is having a profoundly regressive effect on boys.[28] For many of these adolescents pornographic materials are the only form of sex "education." This does not augur well for their relationships with women.

Pornography sets certain standards for what women are for and what they should look like. Any woman who has stolen a glance at her spouse's *Penthouse* has to wonder whether she can live up to what he finds sexy there. She has warts, the pin-up is airbrushed. She has excess pubic hair, the pin-up is smoothly shaven. She wears a B-cup brassiere, while the pornographers have found a way to turn the pin-up's D-cup mammaries into perky perfection. There are reports that women are punished by their spouses for not looking like the women in the pictures, although, of course, nobody really looks like the women in them. Nevertheless, women try to avoid ridicule by experimenting with the practical equivalents of airbrushing — plucking eyebrows, and shedding pounds, trying to conform to pornography's cosmetic identity for women.

Although men have felt that expectations about their sexual performance have increased their anxieties, the social pressure to conform to a single standard is not nearly as heavy for them as for women. Certainly pornographers do not harp on a single standard of male beauty, even taking into account the pornographic insistence that men be controlling and powerful. In *Playboy*, sex researchers Masters and Johnson were interviewed about research they had undertaken with *Playboy* funds. During the interview they were asked to comment on the average penis size. Masters and Johnson flatly refused, worrying that it would have a negative effect on *Playboy*'s readers and that "everyone would walk around with a measuring stick." In the same magazine, *Playboy* merrily announced the measurements of that month's playmate. While these authorities on sexuality nurse the male ego away from fears of impotency, women continue to fret over whether they can cope with the breast fetish *Playboy* and other magazines like it have nurtured for years.

Media products specializing in objectification not only set the standard for what women should look like, but they also set the standards for what women are for: sex. This matters to women in their actual lives. Pick a situation: Will a woman be able to get out of her house to work if her husband thinks she already has a job — sexually servicing him? Can a woman get a raise if all her boss sees when he looks at her is tits and ass? Will she get a raise if her boss gets an erotic charge out of saying no? These questions clarify the way pornography reinforces conditions of inequality, how pornography makes these conditions difficult to change, and why pornography is itself an institution of sexual inequality.

If someone is told one single time that women are naturally

lubricious and enjoy rape, he may not believe it. But if he is told again and again — especially if the information comes from more than one source — the chances of him believing it will be greatly increased. Linda Marchiano told the truth and was not believed. Such is pornography's power of persuasion. A seventy-minute film in which she appeared as an actress, seen in the context of thousands of similar products, was more convincing than her repeated accounts of what happened to her, more convincing than the scars on her body. Pornography thus does more than construct women's image of themselves, it decimates women's credibility.

What it does to sex itself is another distressing matter. Laboratory studies have tested the attitudes of men who have looked at repeated scenarios of the rape myth and compared them with the attitudes of men who had not been exposed. Men exposed to the rape myth believed that women enjoyed rape and sex that was forced on them in significantly greater numbers than those who were not so exposed.[29] Pornography, it seems, has the effect of convincing consumers that women invite sexual advances, that sexual harassment is not harassment and that rape is only good sex preceded by women's sexiest protest: please don't.

This collapsing of rape into sex is also obvious when so many observers have so much difficulty seeing force on the screen when it is obviously there. For example, some researchers continue to refer to a film like *Debbie Does Dallas* as non-violent pornography. What they mean is that their subjects did not *perceive* any violence in it. Yet *Debbie Does Dallas* contains several instances of forced sex, including one in which a woman, presented as a teenager, is held down by the head so that she will fellate the man holding her, and another in which a woman is accosted in the shower by three strangers to whom she eventually submits. The researchers' male subjects don't perceive these scenarios as coercive. The fact that these scenes are not recognized as force attests to how pornography insidously merges forced sex with sex, or the "just sex" that is supposedly acceptable by sexually liberated standards.

Realizing pornography's influence might give a new perspective to a woman who has experienced the "come on you know you love it" style of persuasion from a man who is interested in her and whose persuasion grows less gentle as she resists. It might help the rape survivor understand why her assailant was screaming "this is what you want" throughout the assault. It might even be relevant to rape trials in which juries have trouble understanding why sexual assault, pleasurable according to pornography, is something for which a rapist should be punished.

By making women look like children, and by turning children into an ideal sexual object, pornography promotes the sexual abuse that helps create the population of women who wind up in other pornography somewhere down the line. Pornography supplies child abusers with an entire range of products that make them feel supported, lead them to believe that they are not doing anything wrong, or that *they* could engage in similar acts and not be punished for them. This is the same classic modelling behaviour uncovered in the rape myth studies. So persuasive are the advertisements for child rape that child rapists use them to recruit their victims, showing them or reading them pornographs that raise the issue of sex in the first place and train children in sexual compliance. Many survivors of this experience have described how their later pornographic performances felt like a logical extension of these early assaults.[30] Some have said that they felt a compulsion to continue to re-enact their victimization through performance in pornography. Others who were raped as children and perhaps never photographed wound up in the conditions of prostitution that became the experiential analogue of never having owned their own bodies as children. What happens is that the pornography increases the appeal of child sexual abuse, which is then acted out on children, which in turn helps create the population of women who will wind up in the pornography of the future. Pornography is thus itself a cycle of abuse.

At the same time as pornography merges rape with sex, it has the effect of changing women's status to something less than human. Men exposed to violent pornography tend to trivialize the violence in the films.[31] Crucially, this callousness toward's women's injuries has been shown to cross over into real life. In one study, male subjects were asked to participate in a (mock) rape trial after viewing violent pornography. They failed to see the seriousness of a woman's real rape, and they gave a significantly shorter sentence to the rapist than did men who had not seen the films.[32] Similar studies using the so-called non-violent "just sex" materials have produced similar results.[33] It seems that when men see women engaged in sex, whether forced or apparenty consensual, they think women are inferior and care about them less.

Wishful thinkers, speaking in favour of giving the green light to sexually explicit materials, have argued that pornographers will eventually bore their customers to the point that the industry dies out. Industry profit margins indicate that this is not likely to happen. Critic Robert Fulford has referred to this as the greatest disappointment of our liberal democracy. His view is reminiscent of that of some socialists who wonder why post-revolutionary governments do not simply disappear. The fact is that like the state in the real world of post-revolutionary turmoil, pornography under sexism just will not wither away.

Pornography does not confine its dynamic to men who prey on women or women who are primed for victimization. And so everyone, regardless of expanded consciousness, has had the experience of watching a scenario on television or in the movies in which a man and woman are arguing. The decibel level rises, the woman tries to leave, but as she tries to get past him, he grabs her by the arm and pulls her to him. We automatically assume that things are heating up and that sex is bound to be the consummation of all this aggression. What we expect from this passionate interlude is that the woman in the picture is about to have hot sex. In prime-time fiction, she probably will, but in real life, she will have bruises on her arm. Pornography makes it hard to tell the difference between the two.

When pornography "works" for us, it makes us neither immoral or liberated. Rather, it makes us well-socialized products of a system determined to make sexuality a powerful force for maintaining inequality. The values of sexism then become learned, not just in our heads, but in our bodies. Sexual subordination feels good. It feels good to men to have power over women; coercion feels good, force feels good. The more a woman resists the force, the more erotic the encounter becomes. The new female market for pornography only proves how perfect the system is. Whereas in the past, men got aroused by male domination and female powerlessnes while women remained disinterested, now women can get aroused by female submission and male power over them. Doubtless they have been persuaded that by doing so, they are "exploring their sexuality." But they are not exploring any sexuality that truly belongs to them, they are exploring the sexuality that pornographers have constructed for them. This does not make for political change, it makes for the completion of the pornographic process across sexual lines. By turning men on to putting women down, sex becomes a weapon deployed in maintaining the status quo. Women remain on their knees, while the sexual act is turned into an act of male supremacy. Getting these values into women's heads makes them seem part of nature, rather than part of the social construction of sexuality, a process through which sex itself is made into a weapon for keeping women in their place. One of the profoundly political questions that is central to this exploration is this: In whose interests is it that sex be constructed in this way?

For years feminists have insisted that pornography lies about women, and lies about men too. Women are not this way, feminists insist. Men do not really do these things. But when sexual abuse is so prevalent that women are paralyzed with fear, unable to get on with their everyday lives, worried that looking a man in the eye will be confused with giving him the eye; when it is so easy to eroticize conflict between women and men; when the operative language of sexuality is that men take and women surrender; when assaulted women complain that they have trouble distinguishing between their spouses' controlling behaviour and love; when incest survivors report that they cannot trust their own orgasms; when it becomes clear that pornography is not a fantasy but a practice of sexual subordination; and that this subordination is made sexy so that it will be reproduced, then the reality has to be faced. Pornography is an effective agent of social control, and the lies of pornography are becoming the truth about life.

5

IN 1982 THE WIMMEN'S (SIC) FIRE BRIGADE claimed credit for blowing up three Red Hot Video outlets in British Columbia. The members of the Brigade would be extremely uncomfortable among the devotees of the church, family and decency who have taken a strong stand against pornography. Right-wingers, in turn, would be appalled to discover that their opposition to pornography was shared by anarchists, or worse, lesbian feminists, a group they would be more likely to identify as perverts in cahoots with pornographers than as allies. In the meantime, critics of the feminist anti-pornography viewpoint remain mired in the regrettable fiction that feminists opposing pornography are really Bible-thumpers in extravagant political drag.[34]

There is a good reason why confusion reigns here. Feminists and right-wing groups have been jostling over the same politically charged terrain — family, reproduction and sexuality — for almost a decade. The conservative contingent believes that the family is the backbone of the social order. Representatives of Canadians for Decency, a group of conservatives organizing against pornography, have stated explicitly that they are family people.[35] The family, according to the credo of the conservative, provides a tidy structure in which sexuality, male sexuality especially, can be controlled. Without the family intact, argues the moralist, male sexuality would run rampant, posing a persistent threat to the civilized status quo.[36] Feminists, however, insist that the conservative model for the family, in which women take care of children and the housework while men take care of the real world, is hopelessly undemocratic. Men's work in the real world is paid work and carries with it a great deal more status than housework. When women are locked into unpaid work in the family and depend on husbands for money, they lose their mobility and their autonomy. This does not mean that when women work outside the home, their families suddenly become democratic, for often under those circumstances, women wind up taking on the double role of housekeeper and breadwinner. But the right-wing model for the family based in old traditions is still an institution of inequality.

And far from being a safe place for women, the family winds up being a haven for violent men. New research shows that one out of eight women will be assaulted by the man she lives with. And another Canadian study reports that one of four women will have her first sexual experience under conditions of force, at the hands of a member of her family or someone close to it. The family has been men's private sphere for controlling women without worrying about the long arm of the law. Police are still reluctant to interfere in "domestic disputes" lest they invade someone's privacy. Until 1983, the law gave legal protection to rapists, provided that the assailant was the husband and the victim the wife. In the end, what these protective measures do is keep not sex but sexual abuse in the family.

The right wing believes abortion is the ultimate sin and compulsory pregnancy a suitable punishment for a woman who has been sexually active. The conservative opposition to abortion is closely linked with its moralist stance on sexuality in general: sex should be confined to the marriage contract and private behaviour, and kept away from public view and public discourse. Recreational sex is lust and lust keeps people in chains,[37] binding all to the prison of their bodies, whose appetites have to be kept in constant check. Within this frame, moralists identify men as the weaker sex and more likely to yield to temptation, but it is women who are blamed for tempting them, much the way the pornographer makes women responsible for all sexual excess.

While conservatives have wanted to keep sex private, feminists are making sexuality a political issue. If the forces of decency argue that sex is intrinsically negative and has to be repressed and thwarted, anti-pornography feminists like myself say that society's mass culture — with pornography as one of its most influential instruments — constructs sexuality in a particular way, making it so that women are used or made powerless in the construct of dominance and submission, coercion and violence. If the forces of decency argue that sexuality imprisons us, we would counter that sexuality is not intrinsically or naturally negative. It *has* no nature. Instead, it has to be reconstructed with an entirely new set of values. If we do not allow the pornographer to do all the exploring for us, sexual exploration on our terms — if we can find them — will be a liberating force.

When right-wingers speak, they do so with a wistful nostalgia for a past they believe was much more simple and straightforward. But the past holds no special magic. The western world for generations gone by has not been a particularly hospitable place for women, who could enter the work force only in demeaning low-paid jobs and who were given no role in political life, let alone a sexuality over which they might have had some control. It's a future where women have self-determination that feminists hunger for, and that future *would* include female orgasm.

In the face of these differences, it should come as no surprise that right-wing and anti-pornography feminist views on pornography are not consonant at all. There is only the agreement that pornography has to be fought. Underlying that, there are profound differences on the question of why. In the mind of the conservative, pornography leads to the destruction of the family by providing an outlet for recreational sex and the expression of anti-social sexual values. The anti-pornography feminist believes that the family is quite resilient and that plenty of family men love pornography. As long as the family remains undemocratic, the pornography that promotes the power imbalance between the sexes, and the family that makes a man's home his castle, are two very compatible things, part of the same social order. The way the conservative sees it, pornography excites lust, which leads to pregnancy outside of marriage, which leads to the heinous sin of abortion. But according to the anti-pornography feminist view, pornography enshrines male control over women. This is the same control over women that is exercised when the state refuses to give women access to abortion and reproductive freedom.

Pornography, according to the decency contingent, is a moral outrage depicting recreational sex; God would not want it that way. For anti-pornography feminists, pornography expresses a political fact — the power of men over women. The Lord is not an actor in the scenario except to the extent that he provides a pretext for orthodox churches to repress sexuality while giving women the unenviable choice of being either virgin or whore.

That is why these orthodox churches have never really been able to foil the will of the pornographer: because both the church and the pornographer will their control of women.

Descriptions of this rift between the forces of decency and the forces of feminism tend to put the arguments in their starkest terms, leaving out some of the more intriguing political complexities. The original triumvirate of male villain and male hero battling it out over the right of the average man to masturbate *has* changed in more ways than one. Not just feminists have started to talk about how they feel. Whereas the forces of repression used to be represented by male church leaders, women have become some of the most articulate proponents of the conservative stance.

High-profile political groups like the American Eagle Forum or the Canadian REAL Women have taken positions against pornography. Most of the time these women use the tried and true conservative arguments against public sexuality and threats to the family structure. Most of the time right-wing women think like right-wingers. But some of the time, right-wing women think like women. For example, Nancy Pollack, the president of Canadians for Decency, will say outright that the Bible speaks out against fornication, but she also believes that pornography says something in particular about sex. "Pornography is someone to have, someone to get, someone to do in," she once said. "It's never a mutuality. In the stuff I've seen, the woman is frightened and hates it, then she loves it and that's supposed to be the way it is." Pollack may be a Christian opposed to public sex, but she also knows the rape myth when she sees it.

British Columbian anti-pornography activist Jancis Andrews is another case in point. She undertook a campaign to get the province's attorney general to file obscenity charges against Red Hot Video. During her campaign, she wrote to the provincial ombudsman that "violent pornography is misogyny using video tape as its medium and therefore should be regarded as a form of hate propaganda."[38] In another letter to the attorney general, she wrote that "our work with the porn issue is just part of our fight for the human rights of all people, and when it is over ... we shall see the face of Christ and hear him say, 'Well done thou good and faithful servant.'"[39] What a remarkable hybrid Andrews is — a woman who has a clear understanding of how pornography is used as a weapon to control women, and who awaits the moment of ultimate approval from the heavenly father! Nevertheless, though occasionally Pollack's and Andrews' visions blur around the woman-identified and fundamentalist edges, neither is a feminist. They have accepted the traditional discourse and have located themselves on the side of morality. The alliance between feminists and right-wingers is an illusion.

At the same time as right-wing women have begun to ally with the forces of repression in what was once an entirely male dialogue, so too have women taken the opposing view in the traditional debate, articulating the civil libertarian position.[40] Some of these women proudly identify themselves as feminists and believe they have devised expressly feminist reasons not to oppose pornography. But in the same way as right-wing women sometimes sound more like women than right-wingers when they oppose pornography, libertarian feminists often sound more like civil libertarians than feminists when they defend it. While attempting to give their argument a feminist edge, fundamentally liberal values continue to permeate their discussions.

These values have always been imbedded in the civil libertarian defense of pornography, a defense that rests with the claim that pornography is speech and that speech, especially when it is sexual and thus constitutes dissent, has to be protected and "free" in a democratic society. Anti-pornography feminism challenges all of the elements in this formulation. For when the pornographer is so adept at defining who and what women can be; when he is so convincing as he promulgates the rape myth; when the pictures and words of pornography are there to arouse, and thus make male dominance and female submission seem second nature; when it sexually subordinates women in its production with the expectation that the subordination will continue in the consumption, then pornography is not speech at all. It does something. It is a practice.

Pornographers have been celebrated as freedom fighters because they trade in sex. This exalted status of sexual dissident is closely related to the conviction that society is sexually repressed, and that pornographers, with their open expression of sexuality, are liberators. In other words, it doesn't matter what the pornographer says about sex, it's the fact that he brings sex out into the open that matters. Given the array of cultural products that exploit sexuality and given the popularity of the products of pornography, one has to question the assumption that we live in a sexually repressive culture. Sex manuals and how-to books are voraciously consumed by people anxious to get the sex they believe will confer on them some kind of personal identity. There still is, of course, resistance to gay and lesbian sexuality, but the kind of sex pornographers promote — heterosexual scenarios of dominance, submission and force — are very popular, as we saw from the ease with which these sexual values are mainstreamed.

Some sex liberals[41] insist that pornography is appealing precisely because society is so repressed. Unfetter sexuality, and the pornography will become less ugly, they say. According to this perspective, pornography is a marginalized phenomenon that depends on sexual taboo for its commercial success. But the pornographers no longer depend on taboo to sell their products. Indeed, far from pandering to the repressed conditions that allegedly keep them in business, pornographers have already broken down the barriers of sexual repression and are actually the active and effective agents in the creation of a hypersexualized society.

Ultimately, it does not matter what the pornographer says about sex, for he is decidedly not neutral on sexual values. Rather than resisting the dominant ideologies of our society, pornographers reinforce and construct them by turning the hierarchy of gender into something sexually arousing. Pornography is an institution, itself institutionalizing sexual inequality and other hierarchies, like racism, by eroticizing them. So-called pro-sex advocates who claim to see a range of sexual practices in the products of pornography categorize sadomasochism or elaborate fetishes as sexualities that resist society's prevailing sexual values. But analyzing sexuality in a different way (for more see further), sadomasochistic sexuality is an extreme practice of the very mainstream phenomenon of dominance and submission, and fetishism is but another practice of objectification. Seen this way, pornography does not push the boundaries of sexuality, it keeps them locked within the frame of hierarchy, conflict and violence. Far from being the purveyors of dissent, pornographers are eloquent advocates of the status quo — men on top, women on the bottom, socially and sexually speaking.

Civil libertarians who accept that pornography hurts women still insist that in a free and democratic society, even obnoxious speech has to be tolerated. Deny one person's freedom, and you establish a precedent for denying someone else's. This position is forged out of the fear that if one voice goes, permission is given to deny the voice of dissent. But this point of view assumes that everyone has rights to begin with, when the persistence of pornography proves that not all members of society have equal access to freedom of speech, regardless of the Charter of Rights and Freedoms or any other state guarantees. To give real voice to real speech, people have to have resources, skills, training, and in particular, money. Or as one person put it, the more money you have, the more free speech you can buy.[42] Women do not have as much finanacial clout and access to other resources as men do in a patriarchal system, and part of maintaining that system is making sure that women's access to these things does not increase.

In our political culture, it is the pornographer who builds his empire of propaganda and forced sex while women protest in the face of liberal platitudes. There is a pathetic irony in the fact that the three words that have been used most effectively to subvert women's activism against pornography have been "freedom of speech." And one of the most effective agents in negating women's voice has been the pornographer, who reduces women to objects so that their credibility is undermined. Women are increasingly frustrated with the deep entrenchment of liberal values that assume that just by saying everyone has equal rights, those rights will automatically materialize. The romanticization of free speech and other individual freedoms will never subvert male dominance and will instead continue to buttress existing power structures. Women have to ask: why should we let the pornographer speak when he does so much to keep us silent?

As the forces of repression meet those of expression, one wonders why oppression is left out. While observers, whether male or female, choose up sides in the pornography question, other anti-pornography feminists and I redefine the terms of the debate. The right thinks pornography is a moral issue of good and evil, I see it as a political problem of power and powerlessness.[43] The civil libertarian defends pornography as an idea or speech, I am fighting it as a practice of sexual subordination. The moralist says pornography unbridles male sexuality, I say it directs it. The civil libertarian wants to protect freedom, including the pornographer's. I yearn for the day when women will have freedoms to defend.

Ultimately, by questioning pornography's relationship to women, the feminist arguments wind up cutting through the tension between the two traditional sides of the dichotomy. The right-winger warns that the pornographer poses a danger to ordered society, the civil libertarian defends the pornographer's right to do so, while I insist that the pornographer is the champion of a very ordered status quo. And while the decency contingent fears the pornographer, the liberator, and the civil libertarian defends the pornographer, speaker and dissident, I know the pornographer is a pimp.

CHAPTER II

THE LAW

1. FEMINIST CRITERIA FOR ANTI-PORNOGRAPHY LAW

SINCE FEMINISTS BEGAN TO UNCOVER the harms of pornography and to seek legal strategies against it, we have been asked the same the question over and over again: "Don't we already have laws that deal with the problem?" The answer is yes and no. Yes, we do have what some call the most repressive censorship machinery in any western democracy. But no, we do not have a body of law that addresses the actual harm of pornography.[1]

Canada's anti-pornography laws — specifically obscenity in the Criminal Code, the provincial Theatres Acts and the Customs Tariff — have come under attack from a number of fronts. Most so-called decency groups say that Customs and police officials are not being vigilant enough in implementing the laws we do have. Anti-censorship activists say that Canada's pornography laws are hopelessly vague and far-reaching, snagging in their broad nets almost all sexual representation and any radical explorations of sexuality. Then there are anti-pornography feminists who echo the anti-censorship view that Canada's laws are a danger to sexual expression. But they remain convinced that finding a legal remedy for pornography is a reasonable proposition, provided the laws take on the issue of violence solely and directly.

Along with other radical feminists, I want to add another dimension to these critiques of pornography law. The purpose of this chapter is to explain this new perspective and to see how it can be used to redraft a legal approach. The chapter begins by suggesting seven criteria that I believe have to be met by anti-pornography laws. These criteria encompass feminist values, taking into account the experience women have with pornography and with the legal system. They address the issue of how pornography has to be perceived and defined if the law is to be useful. They also deal with the question of what dynamics make for a law that can provide relief and not repression, and exactly what an anti-pornography law ought to target.

1. *Consider pornography a practice, not merely pictures, words or ideas*

For a long time pornography has been discussed as a two-dimensional artifact. This insistence that it is the picture alone that counts has allowed judges as well as critics of pornography law to argue that individual differences in values or taste make it impossible to set a standard or a definition for what pornography really is.[2] Adding to the problem has been the tendency, especially when the discussion is centered on pictures, for the language of "representation" and "image" to become the operative vocabulary. This has led to the assumption that pornography, the picture or the image, is an idea and that the expression of the idea is fundamental requirement for freedom.[3] But women's experience with the production and consumption of pornography shows that pornography is not a picture at all. It is a practice that involves very specific activities, including trafficking in women, using women without their consent, and physically assaulting women so that a product can be sold. Pornography is made through the sexual subordination of women and cannot exist without it. Pornography is also made so that consumers can experience the sexual subordination that it advertises. This happens when users force the women they know to buy pornography, look at it and/or replicate the activities in the pictures. This is an important dynamic of pornography: its tendency to re-invent itself in the actions of its consumers. Studies have revealed that pornography has an important effect on consumers' attitudes about women and sexuality, and that pornography can desensitize viewers and readers to the violence women experience.

The way pornography is produced, the way consumers use it and the influence the materials have on their attitudes towards women, sexuality and sexual violence are all parts of the pornographic package. Thus pornography is not a two-dimensional artifact, an image or an idea, but a series of activities in which women are used to create materials that will be used to subordinate other women. A law that purports to deal with pornography must deal with all aspects of the pornographic process. A law that does deal with the subordination of women in pornography is less likely to be accused of repressing ideas, for such a law will not be abstract. Instead it would deal with the concrete fact that when pornography exists, people are doing something very particular, usually to women.

2. *Target the harm women experience*

The language of pornography law in both Canada and the United States has been the language of "corruption," "morality" and "decency." These are abstractions constructed on religious conviction or on assumptions about what pornography is doing to the health of society. As long as members of decency groups and even liberal commentators have been concerned about the damage pornography (or in its legal guise, obscenity) does to society, the laws have reflected those concerns. When the real experience of women is left out in the formulations of pornography laws, and the health of body politic becomes the focus instead, the laws tend to be ineffective. Canada's pornography laws were designed for something abstract like the social good and not for something concrete, like the lives of women. Consequently, the laws have not done much to curtail the activities of pornographers, and the pornography industry has continued to burgeon.

3. *Make the law women-centred and not gender-neutral*

Because pornography cannot exist without the subordination of women, a law that purports to address the problem must recognize the gender specificity that makes it possible for pornography to exist. The law has to accept the fact that pornography is not gender-neutral and that women carry an unequal burden of the victimization that occurs in this practice. In some other fields, a gender-neutral law can alleviate women's situation. But in the case of pornography, a practice that is not gender-neutral, a law dealing with the practice cannot be gender-neutral either. Not only is a gender-neutral law unlikely to reach the real harm of pornography, but legal history indicates it also will encourage men to seek whatever relief they can find through the law — a male-dominated justice system makes that inevitable — while women remain silent.

It is my concern with the reality of pornography that makes me wary of an approach that encourages law-makers to legislate against excessive violence in mass media as if this were a strategy to deal with pornography. Targetting violence is a gender-neutral approach, since men are as likely as women to be the victims of violence that is not sexual. There may be some benefits to limiting the amounts of violence on television and movie screens but such initiatives ought not to be confused with anti-pornography strategies, which must target sexual subordination instead. And sexual subordination as it is lived is not gender-neutral.

Radical feminist legal scholars have tried to resist liberal legal strategies that tend to confuse articulating equality rights with creating them. A law that says that the sexes are equal is not the same as a law that actively works to create equality. Indeed, in the United States, liberal equality theory has been used as a weapon *against* legal initiatives that would help women in concrete ways. For example, in the United States, representatives of the National Organization of Women (NOW) intervened *in favour* of a California bank whose lawyers used American equality laws to deny women pregnancy leave. The NOW lawyers argued that giving women these benefits would discriminate against men, which in turn would threaten women's equality rights. This peculiar reasoning created the unseemly spectacle of allegedly equality-minded women allowing the abstract notion of equality to overwhelm the practical need for legal initiatives that can substantially change the power imbalance between the sexes.[4] By saying that if women want equality, they have to pay the price and lose advantages in some areas, such as in pregnancy leave benefits, these liberal thinkers turned equality rights into a form of punishment for women.

When women have paid the price for inequality for so long,

it hardly seems fair to exact a price for equality now. It is also contrary to the spirit of feminist activism to sit by and imagine that equality will miraculously materialize. Some feminist lawyers believe that the equality provisions in the Canadian Charter of Rights and Freedoms can be used to support gender-specific situations, like, for example, women's organizations and women's services such as sexual assault centres. As far as gender-specific laws are concerned, in spite of the Charter's gender-neutral language, there is no existing law and no doctrinal interpretation yet offered by the courts that undermines a gender-specific approach.[5] In fact, precisely because the Charter guarantees sex equality rights, we can begin the process of drafting laws that can help to alter women's status in substantive ways.

I think pornography is one place to test this strategy. Pornography is about sex, about how women are used for sex and about constructing sexual values so that women will continue to be used and abused in sex. Pornography actually genders sexuality itself, so that male sexuality is promoted as dominance over women while female sexuality is promoted as submission to men. Because this is how pornography works, a gender-neutral law would be wholly ineffective in dealing with the problem, while a gender-specific law could actually do something to increase the possibility for real gender equality.

4. *Make the law women-initiated and women-driven*

Most existing pornography law relies on increased powers for law enforcement officers. Increased powers are given to police officers who decide whether criminal charges should be laid; to bureaucrats who decide whether films should be cut and how they should be classified; to Customs officials who determine whether or not materials ought to be allowed into the country. It is true that police sometimes act on the complaints of women, and that the community standards implemented by censor boards and Customs law may take women's interests into account, but in all cases, the final decision as to whether a case goes to court, whether a film gets a commercial release or whether materials are granted entry rests with the traditional authorities. Most of the time, these law enforcement officers, whether police or bureaucrats, are men, so that creating laws that increase their discretionary powers only serves to give the male-dominated justice system more clout that it already has.

More to the point, these arbiters are not necessarily best situated to determine what the harm of pornography really is. Some of them are themselves users of pornography;[6] some of them believe that pornography, unless there are children involved, is a victimless crime; some of them have trouble distinguishing between materials that are harmful and materials that aren't. Some have used laws to harass people who are not pornographers.

Because pornography is active in the subordination of women, the best law against pornography will be a law that empowers women, the ones who are the actual victims. Such a law would give women the choice to take action if they have been victimized in pornography's production or consumption. The matter would not be left open to the interpretation of state authorities who themselves have seldom, if ever, experienced pornography's harm, and who instead are in a position to use pornography law to increase their powers. A law that empowers women would also provide opportunities for women to describe in detail what happened to them and how pornography affected their lives.

No single law can by itself give women equal access to the justice system; even a women-driven law against pornography cannot guarantee that a woman using it will not encounter discrimination in the courts. When I use the term women-driven, I am aware that even if a woman were to make a claim against pornography in her own name and in her own voice, she could encounter sexism in the justice system. But a law can be designed with specifications that give women more room to maneuver and more opportunity to get a full hearing than ever before.

5. *Compensate the victims of pornography*

Creating a law that is women-driven and that gives women a voice and decision-making powers is one way of empowering women in the legal system. Another, equally important empowerment strategy is compensation for women who are the victims of pornography. An effective law against pornography not only allows women to decide whether materials should come under the law, it not only gives the victims the chance to describe in court what the harm of pornography is, but it also does something concrete for those who have suffered.

Historically, pornography laws have not provided many benefits for pornography's victims. Obscenity laws and film censorship may have prevented some subordinating materials from being distributed or sold, which may in turn have limited the deleterious effects pornography has on the status of women in general, but if a woman has been forced into pornography or had pornography forced on her, nothing in the law has made it possible for her to get any relief. Instead, pornographers have been sent to jail, or more frequently, fined for their offenses. In keeping with the law's presumption that pornography harms society instead of women, the money has gone into the government's coffers, instead of into the victim's hands.

A really useful law against pornography would compensate those who are victimized by the sexual subordination on which pornography depends. Only a law that targets pornography's real harm in the first place can reach the harm and aid those who are injured. Only a law that provides compensation for a woman who is hurt can be truly empowering for that woman.

6. *Advance gender equality*

Pornography plays an important role in maintaining women's second-class status. Pornography uses women in sex so that consumers learn that women's worth is in their sexual value alone. This makes it difficult for women to rise above the status of sexual object. Pornography also teaches consumers that men can get pleasure and power from sexually abusing women and that women enjoy the sexual abuse they experience. These dynamics work to guarantee that sexual assault, wife assault, incest and sexual harassment will continue to threaten women's rights to walk the street in safety, to live in their homes without abuse, and to work without fear that they and their work will be sexualized and devalued. The clinical studies of pornography described earlier lead to the disturbing conclusion that pornography desensitizes the consuming population to the meaning and effects of violence in real life. This dynamic makes it more difficult for women to address the issues of sexual abuse socially and legally, and to change the circumstances that make sexual abuse so pervasive.

For these reasons, pornography has to be seen as an issue of sex equality. As long as pornography flourishes it will actively perpetuate women's second-class status and their vulnerability to sexual assault. A law that combats pornography must advance the sexual equality pornography denies.

7. *Permit artistic and educational dialogue on sexuality*

Society is in a sexual crisis that pornography has helped create. The majority of pornography consumers in this country are young male adolescents who are learning lies about what women want. As pornography instills the values of male dominance and female submission, the need for educational materials and initiatives that will foil these values intensifies. The long-term strategy for eliminating pornography is to eliminate the market for it. Artistic and educational endeavours that strive to provide real alternatives to pornography are part of a political and social project to resist pornography by transforming sexuality itself.

Pornography laws must address the harm of pornography without jeopardizing the educational and artistic projects that are committed to social/sexual change. A law that helps women but targets materials that are part of a longer-term strategy against pornography may bring benefits to women in the short run, but in the long run it will seriously damage the movement for changes in sexual attitudes and practice.

2. THE CRIMINAL CODE AND ITS LIMITATIONS

THE OBSCENITY PROVISIONS of the Criminal Code have historically been seen as the most direct way of attacking pornography. But obscenity is a deeply moral concept and that has prevented obscenity law from doing much about the political problem of pornography. The specifically moral framework of obscenity law became entrenched in Canadian law when the first case of obscene libel was adjudicated in 1727.[7] The judge ruled that the peace of society could be disrupted by something other than force — specifically, by an attack against society's morality. In the United Kingdom, the definition of obscenity grew out of censure of public incontinence of various sorts, including written descriptions of sexual intercourse, sexually framed attacks on political figures and disturbances of public order and peace. In an early common law obscenity case, a poem was held to be "a most scandalous, obscene and impious libel."[8]

Between the 1600s and the mid-1900s, the legal definition of obscenity in western legal terms became fairly well-settled, focussing on the notion of "corrupting public morals" — a catch-all formulation that proved to be highly elastic and capable of sustaining varied political interpretations, depending on the social context of the day. In the 1800s, an element of class privilege was grafted onto the law of obscenity, as the combined forces of mass literacy and industrialism raised new concerns about the effects of obscene material on the "propriety" and industriousness of the working class. It is intriguing to note that this was the first context in which there was any concern expressed about the harms of pornography: the literature of the United Kingdom Society for the Suppression of Vice said that pornography caused sex crimes, but only when it fell into the hands of the working class.

Although Canada's jurisprudence in the area was characterized by doctrines and arguments that were specifically moral, a clear legal definition of obscenity was not established until the landmark Hicklin case brought the language of depravity and corruption into the legal arena. If the materials had a tendency to "deprave and corrupt ... minds open to such immoral influences," they were likely to be found obscene.[9] The Hicklin test survived in Canada until 1959, when Section 159 of the Criminal Code was enacted by Parliament. Section 159 stated that "any publication, a dominant characteristic of which is the undue exploitation of sex, or of sex and any one or more of the following subjects, namely crime, horror, cruelty and violence, shall be deemed obscene." In 1962, the Supreme Court held that the new law was to supplant the Hicklin test, and so the "undue exploitation of sex" became the operative legal definition of obscenity.[10]

The history of criminal obscenity litigation is, in many ways, the history of how women's reproductive self-determination and sexuality have been repressed. Since their first enactment, Canada's obscenity provisions have been used to regulate information on birth control,[11] abortion,[12] women's sexuality,[13] alternative sexualities[14] and dissident politics. At the same time, the interpretation of obscenity provisions ensured that men maintained access to women's sexuality in the form of pornography. Sexual material that women would probably have considered degrading or harmful was exempted from liability.

Obscenity doctrine does not ask whether materials under consideration violate women, it asks whether the materials violate Canadian contemporary community standards. The courts have relied on the community standard test ever since its usefulness was argued in 1962[15] and in cases following. The community standard test was designed to avoid circumstances in which judges had to rely on their own personal tastes or on conventional moralist standards to determine whether something was obscene. It has always been important for the community standard to keep up with public opinion. If the prosecution could produce testimony from upstanding community representatives that the materials could not be tolerated by the community, the materials became vulnerable to conviction. Defense lawyers in turn called on their own experts to define community standards and to make the claim that the materials in question would be tolerated, leaving the judge to determine who had the direct line to the community consciousness. According to legal precedent, in borderline cases tolerance was to be chosen over proscription,[16] a ruling that signalled the shift in obscenity law from a conservative single-ethic approach to a more liberal approach favouring freedom of expression.

Against all of the powerful currents driving these new legal initiatives, feminists began to add their voices and opinions to the discourse. This movement began with the declaration that pornography harms women in very specific and particular ways, and that those harms are different from whatever harms have traditionally been associated with obscenity. Instead of focussing on the effects that pornography has on public moral behaviours, public order and speech, or on the way pornography leads to nebulous notions like "corruption" or "depravity," feminists began to talk about how pornography harms women, both directly and indirectly.

When the public protest against pornography began to take shape in the 70s, many feminists studied obscenity law very closely, for the doctrine of obscenity constituted the state's main attempt to come to grips with the flow of pornography. They found that the early cases used the language of morality, which was later replaced by the language of corruption, which finally changed to concerns with the undue exploitation of sex. Feminists noticed then that in spite of changes that appeared on the face of the law, obscenity had never been able to break out of its moral framework. Even in its amended guise, the public display of sex itself was considered problematic, with no reference to what kind of sex was being portrayed, or what effect it may have had on any particular group.

Obscenity's preoccupation with sex, no matter what kind, led feminists to believe that the state was using obscenity law as a means to control sexuality. In particular, it seemed that the law existed for those who wanted to see sexuality tied to marriage and procreation, and who thought that the problem with pornography was that it celebrated some kind of immoral recreational sex. The best testimony to the law's desire to restrict sex to the family was the array of cases in which the distributors of same-sex materials were being charged under Section 159 of the Criminal Code. The number of these cases was disproportionate to the vast quantities of heterosexual pornography on sale.[17]

Although the phrase "undue exploitation of sex" is not exactly eloquent, the legal meaning of Section 159 of the Criminal Code has become established through legal precedent and the shaping of the law in courts, where the meaning of "undue," "exploitation" and "sex" has become quite specific. Between the years 1960 and 1983, the case law focussed closely on sexually explicit activity.

Explicit activity referred to the presentation of an erect penis, sexual intercourse, or any other penetration of any orifice of the body, and as the courts monitored such depictions, the clauses of the law dealing with the combination of sex and cruelty, violence, etc., were almost completely ignored.[18]

It has always been obvious that the definition of sex developed by the courts was very male-centred, establishing the penis as the centre of the sexual universe. The male-centred definition of sex served to protect explicitly violent or aggressive materials that featured women only. I can recall an especially revelatory visit to Project P, the unit of the Ontario Provincial Police mandated to track down pornography distributors. I showed the officers photographs of nude women tied up, bruised and bleeding — photographs plainly marketed for sexual purposes — and asked whether they violated obscenity law. The answer was clear: no, the materials were not obscene.[19] The absence of an erect penis or penetration saved these materials from prosecution. Thus the law permitted women's bodies to be freely displayed, often in brutally subordinating circumstances, as long as a penis was not immediately apparent.[20]

The years between 1978 and 1983 saw the development of a new discourse on pornography and its meaning. The discourse was charged by a growing awareness of nature of the pornography industry, its size and its excesses. In 1977, I was a part of a small group of Toronto women calling themselves Women Against Violence Against Women (WAVAW). WAVAW picketed outside Cinema 2000, where the film *Snuff* was being screened. We suspected that if neither the censor boards nor obscenity law could reach a film like *Snuff*, which advertised the actual murder of a women as an erotic spectacle, then something must be wrong with the law.

In 1983, Judge Stephen Borins handed down a judgement in an obscenity trial that made it plain that the grassroots feminist organizing and the developing feminist critiques of the law had made an impression. In R v. Doug Rankine and Act III Video,[21] Borins deemed eleven out of twenty-five videos he screened obscene. Taking the outrage of women into account, Borins brought the emerging feminist vocabulary into his decision, writing that "... films which consist substantially or partially of scenes which portray violence and cruelty in conjunction with sex, particularly where performance of indignities degrade and dehumanize the people upon whom they are performed, exceed the level of community tolerance."[22]

What made the judgement precedent-setting was the fact that Borins was able to determine that a number of videos unduly exploited sex and violence in spite of the fact that the videos showed no erect penises or penetration. One video, for example, featured a woman masturbating while listening on the phone to another woman who was being tortured and whipped. As well, Borins brought the issues of dehumanization and degradation onto the table. Previously, only sexual explicitness was judged to have vexed the law. But Borins made a point of expressing his concern about the ways in which "most of the films portray degradation, humiliation, victimization and violence in human relationships as normal and acceptable behaviour."[23]

In his judgement, Judge Borins complained that his role as the arbiter of the standard was inconsistent with his role as a judge:

> The judge, who by the very nature of his calling is required to distance himself or herself from society, for the purposes of the application of the test of obscenity is expected to be a person for all seasons familiar with and aware of the national level of tolerance. Thus, the trial judge (or jury) is required to rely upon his or her own experience to decide as best he or she can what most people in Canada think about such material and arrive upon a measure of community tolerance of that material.[24]

While Judge Borins worried about whether the demands of obscenity law were consistent with his responsibilities as a judge, feminists began to point out other problems with the community standard. In her essay "Not a Moral Issue," legal scholar Catharine MacKinnon explains why a legal doctrine that relies on a community standard cannot get to the harm of pornography. In her view, the community standards test makes it seem that the pornographer's crime is that he has found the wrong audience and that if he could only find an audience that would tolerate his excesses, the social contract would be fulfilled.[25]

What does a community standard in a sexist society look like?

Is it something that should be defended? Is it a fair arbiter of what hurts women? The sales figures for mainstream pornography like *Penthouse* and *Playboy* make them the best-read magazines in the country. Maybe *they* reflect the contemporary Canadian community standard. Actually, the presence on the newsstand of materials charged as obscene has been entered as proof that *Penthouse* and *Playboy* did not violate community standards, making the community standards test look exactly like the "marketplace tolerance" defense. The marketplace tolerance defense claims that as long as someone is buying the materials in question, the materials do not violate community standards. This is a defense that completely silences women. The pornography industry is owned and controlled by men who make and sell pornography because male consumers want to have it. When marketplace tolerance is the measure of the community standard, then women have been effectively excluded from that community.

Many anti-censorship feminists worry that an obscenity law based on community standards is bound to target radical and feminist explorations of sexuality. By far the most vulnerable material has been same-sex sexual materials. In fact, the first case of obscene libel in Canada, tried in 1727, involved a book about lesbian love in the convent.[26] In the modern era, especially since 1962, there have been a disproportionate number of charges laid against gay sexual materials. This imbalance can be attributed directly to the community standards test, which in a homophobic society is bound to be violated by same-sex materials.

Gay male materials have been hit hardest, but pornographic versions of lesbianism have also come under the law. It is interesting to note that *Penthouse* first encountered Canada's obscenity laws in 1977 when it featured two women in lesbian sexual situations as the male editors imagined them.[27] With all of *Penthouse*'s misogyny, with its increasingly violent imagery, with its commoditization of women's bodies and its objectification of women in general, it was a lesbian image that vexed the obscenity standard.

Because police, usually men, are not the best situated to determine whether materials are harmful to women, their assessments are not always accurate. In fact they sometimes work to harass activists for social change who want to transform sexual values and not use sexuality to degrade and subordinate. This turned out to be the case in the trial of Marc Glassman, the owner of Pages bookstore in Toronto and the exhibitor of a display entitled "It's a Girl." The display was put together by a feminist art collective called Woomers and featured the found art of sanitary napkins, diapers and other artifacts intended to convey the iconography of being female. The sanitary napkins galvanized Toronto police and led to a formal charge that Pages was exhibiting a disgusting object in a way prohibited by a subsection of Section 159 of the Criminal Code.[28]

The case was especially intriguing because it showed how sexual representations designed to challenge sexist social norms violate community standards. In the end, the artists were frustrated by having to make the claim in court that their art did not violate the standard, when in fact they had created the piece precisely to challenge the status quo. But more important was the fact that the police had been so exercised by the painted sanitary napkins. It is even possible that the police thought they were covered in real blood, not painted. Would women have been so vexed? Probably not. Was the exhibit causing harm to anyone? Not really. But it did come under the fire of the law. A law that was women-initiated would likely never have targetted the feminist art display.

While judges like Stephen Borins began to take seriously feminist concerns about the invulnerability of many sexually violent materials to the law, other judges began to address the other half of the problem with obscenity: the law's targetting of sexual materials, even when the materials depicted consenting adults. Judge J. Shannon of the Alberta Queen's Court Bench distinguished between three different kinds of materials — violent; non-violent but degrading and dehumanizing; and erotica — and provided a detailed description of each. Citing the social science data we surveyed earlier, he held that the Canadian community standard would tolerate erotica. In the face of growing concern about how vulnerable lesbian and gay materials had been to homophobic community standards, Judge Shannon allowed that a film that depicts consenting homosexual adults is not obscene.[29] It was a precedent-setting case that will doubtless be cited in defense of same-sex materials. During the same period, a Manitoba judge delivered a landmark decision that also stated unequivocally that as long as a film showed consenting adults engaged in non-violent sexual acts, that film was not obscene.[30]

Obscenity doctrine in Canada has experienced some dramatic changes. It began as an assault on materials alleged to affect public morals or to contribute to corruption and depravity. By the 60s, the language of the law had lost its Victorian ring but it had been replaced by legal interpretations that continued to reflect the law's discomfort with explicit sexuality. The interpretation of Section 159 of the Criminal Code continued to be male-centred, as judges defined the undue exploitation of sex in male terms, while many depictions of sexual violence managed to stay outside of the law's reach. Feminist critiques of these legal impulses, especially the law's preoccupation with sex, its avoidance of sexual violence and its tendency to attack same-sex materials, have led to an increase in the consciousness of judges and some important changes in the way obscenity docrine has been interpreted.

Since 1978, when women first began to protest against pornography, a number of large and influential Canadian groups have made a concerted effort to stop the proliferation of pornography. These groups include the guardians of morality like Canadians for Decency, moderate feminist and community organizers like the Canadian Coalition Against Media Pornography (CCAMP), and radical feminist groups like Women Against Violence Against Women. These groups speak with different voices but all three have raised problems with obscenity law. The decency contingent complained that the law's teeth were not sharp enough, that the laws were there to attack public displays of sexuality and that police were not vigilant enough in their implementation of the law; CCAMP complained that the teeth of obscenity dug too sharply into sexuality and ought to home in on sexual violence; and feminists looking for legal strategies that reached the real harm of pornography suspected that as long as judges were looking solely at the pictures and not at the entire process of production and consumption, the law had built into it a fundamental flaw.

With this chorus of voices criticizing existing Criminal Code legislation, the Progressive Conservative government drafted Bill C-54 in 1987 in an effort to respond to all parties. The bill attempts to make the legal distinction between erotica and pornography. It defined erotica as visual matter of which a dominant characteristic is the "depiction in a sexual context or for the purpose of sexual stimulation of the viewer, of a human sexual organ, a female breast or the human anal region." Presumably, what is referred to here are the mainstream pornography publications like *Penthouse* and *Playboy*. Possession of erotica is punishable under the new law only if the materials are shown to persons under 18 years of age.

For the definition of pornography, Bill C-54 takes the laundry-list approach. Pornography is any visual matter that shows:

> i. sexual conduct referred to in any of subparagraphs (ii) to (vi) and that involves or is conducted in the presence of a person who is, or is depicted as being or appears to be under the age of eighteen years or the exhibition for a sexual purpose of a human sexual organ, a female breast or the human anal region of, or in the presence of a person who is, or is depicted as being or appears to be under the age of eighteen years.

> ii. a person causing, attempting to cause in a sexual context, permanent or extended impairment of the body or bodily functions of that person or any other person.

> iii. sexually violent conduct, including sexual assault and any conduct in which physical pain is inflicted or apparently inflicted on a person or any other person in a sexual context.

> iv. a degrading sexual act in a sexual context, including an act by which one person treats that person or any other person as an animal or object, engages in an act of bondage, penetrates with an object the vagina or anus of that person or any other person or defecates, urinates or ejaculates onto another person whether or not the other person appears to be consenting or any such degrading act, or lactation or menstruation in a sexual context.

> v. bestiality, incest or necrophilia or

> vi. masturbation or ejaculation not referred to in paragraph iv. or vaginal or oral intercourse.

Anyone who deals in pornography is guilty of an offense.

Plainly the drafters were influenced by critics of every stripe. The decency contingent, as evidenced by the clear proscription of all sexually explicit depictions, including oral and vaginal intercourse, seem to have made the most headway. Even anti-censorship voices were heard, albeit in the most backhanded way, for certainly with its detailed descriptions of which depictions violate the law, the draft legislation is not vague. And the use of words like "degrading" and "impairment," coupled with the law's attention to sexual violence, indicates that feminists were listened to. But the law does not make the feminist distinction between erotica and pornography. The feminist distinction, defined in a number of papers on the subject,[31] is made on the basis of women's experience: pornography is subordinating, erotica reinforces mutuality. Bill C-54 defines erotica as the depiction of human genitalia, a definition that hinges on male experiences with so-called girlie magazines and which defines erotica simply as a milder form of pornography. Had the drafters considered women's experience, they would have understood that erotica and pornography can stand in contradistinction, and are not simply matters of degree.

Taking into account the dramatic changes obscenity law has undergone, and considering that Bill C-54 was designed to respond to public pressure concerning the limits of obscenity, how do these Criminal Code strategies stand up when the seven feminist criteria for anti-pornography law are applied to them? Not very well.

In order for a law to reach the real harm of pornography, it must be concrete. It must consider the activities of people and not the interpretation of pictures. If pornography is considered just a two-dimensional artifact, the legal discourse will focus on philosophical questions concerning personal taste and the meaning of representation, rather than who is getting hurt by whom. Previous passages detailed many of the abuses that occur in the production of pornography — coercion and the use of photographs without the subjects' consent, to name just two. Linda Marchiano's story of being pimped and brutalized in the making of the film *Deep Throat* is a very important example. It helps us understand that many of the abuses of pornography are invisible, for *Deep Throat*, the single most commercially successful pornographic film ever made, looks on its face like a comedy featuring consenting adults.

The dangers of perceiving pornography only in terms of the pictures or the prose it markets were revealed in the important obscenity case adjudicated by Judge Ferg in Manitoba, the same landmark case referred to earlier in which the judge ruled that depicting consensual sex did not violate the obscenity standard. The film in question was *Deep Throat*. The case made it clear not only that obscenity law does not consider pornography a practice, but that in failing to do so, the law continues to protect materials that have been very hurtful to individual women.

Even more than obscenity, Bill C-54 keeps the legal discussion tied to the pictures themselves. A good indication of the moralist framework of the law is the use of the term "degrading" to describe the act of ejaculating on a woman's body. It is true that ejaculation outside of the vagina is a pornographic convention designed most of the time to give the impression that women exist for sex and ought to be discarded after use. But ejaculation onto a woman's body does not have to be degrading. It *could* also be a method of birth control. But Bill C-54 pays no attention to context, to the way pornography is made or what happens when it is consumed. Instead, the explicit and specific list of proscribed depictions makes it abundantly clear that if any of the listed acts are depicted, no matter the way or the context, materials run the risk of being legally assessed as pornography.

The framework of obscenity law is moral. It does not concern itself with political questions of power and powerlessness, it concerns itself with good and evil, and with values regarding what is the appropriate venue for sexual explicitness. This moral framework keeps pornography's real victims invisible, for embedded in the doctrine is the notion that pornography harms society, when in fact it supports society's sexist status quo and its social norms regarding women's second-class status. Women are kept powerless by pornography, and pornography law should address that directly.

As for Bill C-54, it is based more on the decency contingent's opinions about morality than on women's experience of harm. That all forms of sexual activity are included in the bill indicates that the bill is meant to target public displays of sexuality of all kinds. The bill does not focus on violent or degrading pornography, and instead collapses all sexual behaviours under one pornography category. Removing "lactation" and "menstruation" from subsection iv. and deleting clause vi., which makes depictions of masturbation, vaginal, anal and oral intercourse pornography, decreases the dangers of the bill's breadth. But in the main, the drafters seemed to have been more interested in removing images that offended moralists' sensibilities than in taking action against materials that hurt women.

There is nothing in obscenity doctrine that recognizes that women bear more of the burden of pornography's victimization than men. On its face, the law is gender-neutral, leaving the question of who is hurt by pornography open to the interpretation of judges. They in turn have proved the folly of a gender-neutral law by ignoring women's pain and concentrating on preventing the penis from being displayed in sexually explicit scenarios.

Similarly, there is nothing in Bill C-54 that recognizes women's specific place in pornography, except to the extent that it identifies women's bodily functions, lactation and menstruation specifically, as pornographic if they're depicted "in a sexual context." In fact the pornography of menstruation and lactation can be extremely subordinating, depicting women who are degraded by having menstrual blood smeared on them to give the appearance of having been hurt, or showing women lactating in pain for the benefit of the dominant male in the scenario. But the phrase "in a sexual context," which is supposed to be the clarifying qualifier, is not at all eloquent. It is a phrase never before used in pornography law. It has no legal meaning and offers no legal guarantees.[32]

A law that is women-initiated would give women a voice they do not have in current pornography law. Because any Criminal Code strategy leaves the implementation and voicing of pornography's meaning up to police authorities and not to women, obscenity does not meet the feminist criteria for a women-driven law, and Bill C-54 provides no improvements in this area.

Distributors of obscene material either go to jail or pay fines into government coffers. Since the government is in no way harmed by pornography (indeed some high-ranking cabinet ministers have had *Playboy* playmates raise funds for their political campaigns), these penalties do not in themselves provide very many social benefits. Certainly, women are not compensated in any way when the police use the full force of the Criminal Code. Like obscenity law, Bill C-54 is not couched in terms of how women are hurt and instead puts pornographers in jail or fills the state treasury with pornographers' fines.

When materials are found obscene, distributors are informed of the decision and told that the materials have to be removed from retail stores. Since pornography has a profound influence on how women are seen and how sexuality is experienced, its pervasiveness does affect women's status in society and the way sex is used against women. So, decreasing the amount of pornography that exists does in some way remove barriers to women's equality. But practically speaking, police are never in a position to survey every video outlet in the country to make sure offending materials are off the shelves. Thus the single virtue of obscenity law — its ability to decrease the availability of pornography — is not significant in practice.

Even if police were able to monitor the situation closely, such vigilance does not actively advance equality or remedy existing inequalities. Creating a law that is women-initiated and thus enhances women's access to the courts and to freedom of expression in the legal system begins to rectify imbalances. Providing financial compensation to victims of pornography does something concrete to offset the economic deprivation women experience. This economic inequality exists in part because of pornography's message that women exist for sex and not for any other kind of work that gives them dignity and financial security. Obscenity law's ability to advance equality, if it exists at all, is passive, not active.

Bill C-54, with the references to menstruation, lactation, oral, anal and vaginal intercourse removed, could have the effect of limiting the visibility of pornography that eroticizes sexual abuse. This in turn could minimize the attitudinal changes toward women that pornography promotes. But the drafters of Bill C-54 have not considered pornography an equality issue.

The Criminal Code states specifically that obscene material can be shown for educational purposes or to raise consciousness about the content and meaning of pornography. But as long as obscenity targets sexually explicit materials, sex education materials showing penetration can still come under the law. In addition, as long as obscenity targets sexually explicit materials, no matter what their message or dynamic, any explorations of sexuality ran the risk of being charged as obscene material. The more progressive feminist-influenced judicial decisions have eased the situation somewhat, but there are no guarantees that students of sexuality and artists committed to transforming sexual values will not be charged with breaking the law. The sexual explorations needed to resist pornographic values are too important to be put at risk by a law that is so lacking in so many ways.

This question is more complex than the debate on the law has made it. Artists and librarians have been lobbying vociferously against Bill C-54, making the claim that the law is a frontal assault on sexual representation, that it will empty libraries of valuable literature and consign all educational and artistic initiatives on sexuality to obscurity. My concern takes me in the opposite direction. The artistic merit defense has been used successfully in scores of American obscenity cases in which bona fide pornographers were on trial.[33] Why should we leave this defense open to pornographers in Canada? More to the point, why protect art and not women? If materials are degrading to women, or show women being impaired, damaged or maimed in sex, and if they are not educational materials devised to show the excesses of pornography and even if they are created by artists, why should their artistic merit make them less vulnerable to a law? What is it about art that makes it more important than women? While anti-censorship activists worry that sexually explicit depictions will never see the light of day because of Bill C-54, the more pressing concern is that Bill C-54 will allow pornographic art to flourish.

Some feminists have suggested that the way to deal with Bill C-54 is to remove all the sections of the law that do not address specifically degrading and violent pornography. While this approach sounds appealing at first, taking action on it would leave us with a law that does not do much to dismantle the pornography industry. For most pornography is not the obviously violent kind. The photographs of Vanessa Williams published in *Penthouse* were not violent, but the use of them was a violation. The home-made pornography produced at the expense of women who do not want to be photographed is usually not violent, but the women are violated in its production. Most pornography uses the women who have the least money, the least choice — in short, the least power — and puts them in sexual scenarios that appear to be consensual. Much of the pornography used by consumers to humiliate and disempower women is not what Bill C-54 calls violent and/or degrading. Yet the issue of the so-called non-violent pornography is too complex to be entrusted to the courts in the form of obscenity law or Bill C-54. The legislation should be opposed as it stands. It puts alternative erotica at risk and it gives police increased powers. We have to look for legislation that fits our seven feminist criteria, and Bill C-54 — like the obscenity law it is supposed to replace — fits none of them.

Although the Criminal Code fails to meet feminist criteria, a law that restricts the distribution of violent pornography would be somewhat useful. This type of law is unlikely to be abused by judicial authorities, since "violent pornography" is the kind of term men in decision-making positions understand. In fact, outside the legal context, I define violent pornographs as the materials which men look at and *do* see harm done. They see the harm because if whatever happened to the women in the materials happened to them, they would hurt too. So if a woman is cut and there is blood drawn they can see that yes, that hurts. Legally speaking, this idea turns into a very narrow definition of violent pornography. It does not include a great deal of pornography that *is* subordinating: rape myths are not included because they are invisible to so many men; much of the "just sex" pornographs that promote force are not included because most men do not see force when they look at them, they see sex. It might not even include sadomasochistic scenarios and bondage themes in which women appear to enjoy the abuse, because as long as women smile, men tend not to see the harm.

The definition of violent pornography would wind up applying only to scenarios depicting women in painful situations of torture. The section of Bill C-54 referring to materials which present permanent or extended impairment of the body and bodily functions comes close to encompassing the definition of violent pornography used here. By using such language in the Criminal Code, the law can target the worst pornographic excesses. This will not severely threaten the pornography industry. Nor is it the ultimate strategy for empowering women. But it could have the effect of alleviating women's worse fears, by articulating a clear opposition to the practice of turning the gross violation of women into a profit-making amusement.

3. CUSTOMS INITIATIVES: DO THEY MEET THE CRITERIA?

BECAUSE 97 PER CENT of the pornography available in Canada is imported from other countries, mainly the United States, the provisions of the Customs Tariff have been an important instrument for controlling the flow of pornography across the Canadian border. According to the report of the Fraser Committee on Pornography and Prostitution, the federal government's 1985 public inquiry, Customs officials turned back approximately 7,700 publications between 1978 and 1982.[34] Customs' legal authority to bar entry to these materials is stated in Tariff Item 99201-1 (RSC 1970) of the Customs Tariff, which says that it is illegal to import a publication that is "immoral or indecent." Through case law, "publication" has come to include books, pictures, films, videos and even some sexual aids. Although the language of the Tariff reflects the same morality base as obscenity law, the actual legal test has not been exactly the same.[34]

The Customs Tariff accounts for the only prior restraint implemented at the federal level. Prior restraint refers to any censorship that takes place before the materials in question have been released to the public. When the Charter of Rights and Freedoms was enacted, anti-censorship activists were quick to test the constitutionality of the Customs Tariff. The court ruled that a Customs provision per se did not violate the freedoms of the Charter but that the specific Tariff in operation — especially the words "immoral and indecent" — was too vague and had to be made more specific.[36] Parliament quickly passed emergency legislation known as Memorandum D9-1-1, that provided yet another exhaustive list of depictions which, if present in a publication, would prevent it from being allowed into the country.

The Memorandum, even more so than Bill C-54, takes a bit from every anti-pornography perspective. It begins by stating that any material that might be deemed obscene should be barred entry. The use the word "might" is significant. Customs officials do not confine their restrictions to materials that have already been found obscene in the courts. They have the authority to keep materials out they believe might violate the obscenity standard. Thus we have the predictable restrictions against sexually explicit materials. The Memorandum goes on to list other specific sexual acts that are prohibited, including depictions of bondage and portrayals or descriptions of the act of buggery (sodomy). The Memorandum also includes a clause that is almost an exact replica of feminist Helen Longino's definition of pornography: "materials that depict or describe sexual acts that appear to dehumanize or degrade any of the participants."[37]

Customs regulations allow the head of Prohibited Importations, a department of Canada Customs, to meet with legal counsel for magazine distributors to review upcoming publications and to suggest changes that will ease the publications' entry into Canada. Every month lawyers file into the offices of Revenue Canada, where they are told which depictions would make the magazine unimportable, whereupon the publishers make the appropriate changes so that the magazine can be sold in Canada. Usually these changes are related to portrayals of explicit sex, which are often concealed by the application of black dots to the page, usually at the point of penetration. Sometimes though, these cosmetic changes are not sufficient and publishers have to replace entire pages or photo features with material that will pass the Customs test.

Because the moralist basis for the Customs Tariff, evident in the original law's explicit language of decency and morality, missed the real problems of pornography and because a single moral standard in a Judeao-Christian culture tends to be violated (at least in the minds of judges) by same-sex activities, feminists tended to approve of the court ruling that forced Parliament to dispense with the Tariff Item 99201-1 and to develop specific guidelines for Customs officials. But the new Memorandum continues to pose all kinds of problems for lesbian and gay materials. Between 1986 and 1988 Customs officials seized close to 2,000 magazines and books, including *The Joy of Gay Sex* and other sex education materials.[38]

The basic problem is that the law looks at the pictures, words and ideas and not at the context in which the pictures are presented. For example, paragraph 4(a)(8) of Memorandum D9-1-1 proscribes portrayals or descriptions of the act of buggery. This not only makes it impossible to portray the basics of gay male sex, but it also has seriously threatened important sex education materials designed to reduce the spread of AIDS. One incident in particular shows the way Customs practices bar important educational material, leaving subordinating materials untouched. A publication called *Patches*[39] featured a readers' forum. One reader described how he had performed fellatio "devotedly" on his hands and knees, and ended with the statement that his partner was "the boss" and that "cocksucking was (the writer's) lot in life." The next reader asked for information about how to have safe anal sex. After Customs had reviewed the magazine and suggested changes, the editor's accurate answer about how to have safe sex was cut out: it provided a detailed description of anal sex and how to use sexual aids safely. On the other hand, the paean to sexual subordination presented by the first reader remained intact.

Although Customs has made close to 8,000 seizures over a five-year period, its sweep is actually not very wide. A great deal of pornography is not imported in a way that guarantees an encounter with a Customs representative. Some pornography comes into the country on video via satellite and is re-recorded in Canada. Also, Customs has only joint jurisdiction with Canada Post over international mail and no jurisdiction over telephone communications. By this point the technology exploited by non-Canadian pornographers is far too complex for Customs officials to reach all the product that is available.

Even without these technological advances, Customs officials examine very few imports. It is not the case that every item comes under the watchful eye of Customs. In some cases, officials agree to allow entry to sexually explicit videos, provided that the importer agrees to submit the videos to the appropriate Theatres Branches. But there is no way to ensure that pornographic videos and films are not being copied en masse before they ever reach the censors' screening rooms. As a result, thousands of pornographic titles slip into the country every year.

Despite the fact that the Memorandum's laundry list contains some feminist definitions of pornography, the Customs Tariff was not designed to take into account women's experience. The language of morality is gone, but the influence of the moralist stance is still evident when the Memorandum places in jeopardy all sexually explicit materials. Even the feminist components of the law are gender-neutral. Helen Longino's definition of pornography incorporated in the Customs memo refers to scenarios of sex which degrade the "any of the participants," with no recognition that women carry the weight of pornography's impact. The definition is administered by Customs officials who use their discretion to decide whether materials ought to be admitted into the country. Unless the official is a woman, women are absent from the process, and even if the Customs official is female, she represents the interests and tendencies of the law, not of women as a group.

The Customs Tariff is meant to be a barrier to imported products. It makes no reference to why or to whose interests are served by its administration. It neither mentions victims nor compensates them. Furthermore, by allowing the Tariff to apply to sex education books which have the potential to transform sexual values, the law winds up threatening sexual equality. Certainly the law makes no mention of women's equality interest or the need to limit pornography so as to improve the status of women. And as long as the law targets obscene material and as long as obscenity is defined as sexual explicitness, the Tariff shares all the problems of the current Section 159 of the Criminal Code, and it will continue to put barriers on sex education materials as well as artistic initiatives in the area of sexuality. A law that looks at guidelines and then rigidly applies them to pictures will continue to operate in a way that targets same-sex materials or jeopardizes sex educational materials. A law that looks at the *practice* of pornography could never pose a threat to AIDS-related materials or to sex education initiatives.

In spite of the weaknesses in Customs administration, a strong Customs Tariff on pornography is an important barrier to the flow of pornography into Canada. It is disturbing that Customs officials have targetted gay materials and are harassing lesbian and gay bookstores. But the Customs problem forces us to deal with some hard issues: had the 7,700 titles kept out of the country by Customs been allowed into Canada, then bookstores, video stores and film houses would have looked different and women's lives would have been more stressed. The American pornography lobby is strong and aggressive and is always looking for new markets. Canada, by dint of its proximity to the United States, is a prime target, and if the pornographers are allowed free rein, this country will be inundated with their products. But saying this is not the same as supporting the excesses of Customs administration as it exists. If a Customs Tariff is to remain in place, it has to define pornography in a way that can get to materials that are pornographic, it has to end its harassment of same-sex materials and it has to be implemented consistently across the country.

4. THE FAILURE OF FILM CENSORSHIP

FILM CENSORSHIP HAS BEEN THE SUBJECT of intense debate in Canada for almost as long as moving pictures have existed. All of Canada's provinces have instituted censor boards through their Theatres Acts. Only Manitoba's is not empowered to cut films before they are screened publicly. The rest of the provincial boards can refuse to grant films public screenings. The extent to which the boards exercise these powers depends on political climate and the membership of the board. At this time, Quebec makes the least eliminations, with British Columbia following close behind. Alberta and Ontario regularly cut films and the rest of the boards usually receive their films pre-cut by these provinces.

Discussion here focusses on the activities of the Ontario Film Review Board, for several reasons. First, editions of films shown in Saskatchewan, the Atlantic provinces and the Territories usually originate at the Ontario Film Review Board, making Ontario's the most influential board in the country. Second, Ontario makes the most frequent movie eliminations, on the basis of the presumed social good that will be served by censorship. The third reason, related to the second, is that the major Charter challenges to the legitimacy of film censorship have been launched against the Ontario Board and thus the legal doctrine has been developed on Ontario's terrain.

The Ontario government passed its first Theatres and Cinematographs Act in 1911. Fearing the impact of the thrilling new medium called cinema, the government granted unprecedented powers to George Armstrong, Ontario's first censor. Censors were immediately empowered to cut films if they beieved they went beyond the standards of normal Ontario audiences. What made the dynamic of film censorship different from the legal dynamic of obscenity was the Theatres Act's enactment of a form of prior restraint. Censor boards were given the power to tamper with films before they reached the public, whereas the Criminal Code's obscenity law was applied only to materials that were already in distribution. In 1946, the Ontario censor board added film classification to its duties. Free speech advocates were furious but they did not have enough influence at the time to create a wide debate.

But that changed in the 60s during the regime of O.J. Silverthorn. Silverthorn's belief that film ought to entertain and do little else created a serious rift between the film community and the censors. The gulf widened when the Japanese art film *Woman of the Dunes* came under the censor's knife, and the gulf became a deep chasm when Silverthorn was succeeded by Don Sims. Sims liked to keep the Board's policies and practices private. When

Mary Brown assumed the role of Board chair in 1980, she quickly set about improving the image of the Theatres Branch. Her first gesture was to publicize information about the eliminations the Board was making in films, and she later went on to institute an appeal procedure for exhibitors who were dissatisfied with Board decisions. Throughout, the guidelines for film eliminations, based on the ever-elusive community standard and/or precedents set by obscenity law, remained dangerously vague.

Brown's initiatives did not impress the Ontario Film and Video Appreciation Society (OFAVAS), which was founded to oppose film censorship at the provincial level. In 1982 OFAVAS decided that it would test the constitutional legitimacy of the powers of the Theatres Branch in court. The ruling of the High Court of Ontario in this important case conceded the battle to OFAVAS but the war to the censor boards. OFAVAS hoped that the court would rule that the censor boards violated the principles of the Canadian Charter of Rights and Freedoms, but the court held that of itself, prior censorship of films can be justified in a free and democratic society.[40] The ruling did, however, state that the Board's *guidelines* were not constitutional and would have to be made much more precise in order to pass muster.

The Ontario Ministry of Commercial and Consumer Affairs, under whose jurisdiction the Theatres Branch operates, drafted Bill 82, which clarified specific guidelines for film exhibitors and was passed in 1984. According to this law, all film *and* video — Bill 82 expanded the Board's powers to include jurisdiction over the public exhibition of videos — must be submitted to the Theatres Branch for licence approval and classification if public exhibitions are intended. In addition, the new guidelines for film elimination attempted to provide yet another exhaustive catalogue of depictions deemed in obscenity cases to have offended the Canadian community standard.

Once again, depictions of erect penises and penetration head the list of scenes bound to be cut by the Board. Before Bill 82 came into effect, the censor boards added to the standard of obscenity their own version of community standards. These were assessed mostly on the basis of what kind of mail came into the Theatres Branch from concerned citizens. Accordingly, the censor board included gratuitous violence and sexual scenes that used children among those scenarios that would wind up on the cutting room floor. Under the new regime, depictions of violence against women and degrading sexual acts led to an "R" rating for films, which restricts audiences to those age 18 or over.

In 1980, the National Film Board's anti-pornography film *Not A Love Story* was refused a license for public screenings because it contained sexually explicit scenes that would have been found obscene under the Criminal Code. This decision was made in spite of the fact that the scenes were included in the film to offer examples of pornographic excess, not to celebrate them or to titillate audiences. But there was no room in the Board's guidelines to consider context or intent, and consequently, *Not A Love Story* was allowed only private screenings. In spite of this, *Not a Love Story* remains the most widely screened NFB film in Ontario. The amended Theatres Act did nothing to ameliorate the problems the censor board was having with context. Shortly after it was passed into law, the radical feminist film *Born in Flames* was refused a public screening because it contained a five-second shot of an erect penis being fitted with a prophylactic. The sequence was supposed to make the point that a woman's work is never done, but the Board was not prepared to take context into account. Another sequence, featuring an army of women on bicycles blowing whistles to subvert a rape attempt, fell under the Board's arbitrary category "threat of rape" and led to an "R" classification for the film. The scene, an empowering one for women, would have been entertaining and educational for anyone under the age of 18. But the Board's rigid insistence on looking only at what is in the picture instead of the meaning of the picture caused problems for a film that was an important feminist statement.

The experiences of the National Film Board with *Not a Love Story* and of DEC Films with *Born in Flames* illustrate the ways in which film censorship can hurt women's art. Still, some anti-censorship activists overstate the case. It is not true that feminist and radical materials are the "first to go" when censors are allowed to operate. A brief visit to the Theatres Branch to view the Board's grisly loop of film eliminations will make it plain to anyone that the Board is very preoccupied with pornography and that independent films on sexual politics simply get caught in the crossfire. Still, I have to agree that the Theatres Branch's arbitrary guidelines, its refusal to take context into account, and the focus on explicit sex it shares with obscenity law, have made non-pornographic and feminist film very vulnerable.

A random sampling of censored pornography shows how the dynamics that change consumers' attitudes and lead them to trivialize women in real life remain unchanged after the censors cut pornography. A woman on her hands and knees is begging for sex in a sequence that celebrates her sexual slavery. Eliminating the few frames in which she is penetrated does not change the message. In another scenario, a woman is sexually harassed by her teacher until the harassment is instantly transformed into her sexual pleasure. The scene featuring penetration is cut but the promotion of sexual harassment and abuse is still there.

Independent filmmakers and distributors, who are the most likely to produce progressive film and video, are severely stressed by the demands of the Theatres Act. Films have to be shipped to the Theatres Branch at the distributors' expense and fees have to be paid to the censor board for its "services." These expenses drain the resources of independent distributors and exhibitors. The law indirectly limits the ability of independents to bring to the screen films and videos devoted to social change, and at the same time leads to increased centralization of film distribution in Canada. The pornography industry, on the other hand, is not especially bothered by the law because its resources are so vast. Pornographers continue to ship their products to the Theatres Branch just as long as censorship facilitates the process of getting the pornography into the film theatres, or more likely, onto the shelves of video stores across the province.

The Film Review Board's repeated refusal to consider context, who has produced the films and why, is the clearest indication that the Theatres Act is determined to look only at the pictures, words and ideas of pornography, and not what actually happens to the women presented in the products. The reality is that por-nographers make millions of dollars setting women up as sex in scenes of painful penetration or violence, and then simply clip the scenes before sending the materials over the Canadian border. The Board's demand that sexually explicit scenarios be deleted has not stopped women from being subordinated so that pornography can be made. In fact, the women in the pornography are not recognized by the law. Women continue to be used to make pornography and the women abused by consumers are a factor only in the vague implication that pornography has to be censored because it has an effect on the viewer. Certainly, victims are not compensated by censorship.

While film censorship does almost nothing for women, it does, ironically, do a great deal for pornographers. By demanding that scenarios that might violate the Criminal Code be cut from pornography, the censor board actually winds up protecting pornographers from criminal prosecution by doing the pornographers' clean-up work for them. As well, pornographers do not think of themselves as artists who are violated by the state's censorship demands. They never complain about censorship decisions: in fact they collaborate, facilitating the censorship process when they clip offending scenes before taking the films to the censor boards.

Because the Film Review Board's decisions rely on community standards, the Theatres Branch has become sensitized to the public's desire to regulate the amount of violence that is portrayed on screen. The issue of violence in film is a gender-neutral one. Victims are as likely to be men as women, and even though the perpetrators are more likely to be men than women, the dynamic is much less gendered than pornography, whose purpose is to give men access to female sexuality. Generally speaking, there is nothing in the language of the Theatres Act that notes the special needs of women or the importance to women's lives of controlling pornography. The law is administered by bureaucrats appointed by the provincial government, often in return for political services rendered. The fact that woman-centred films like *Not a Love Story* and *Born in Flames* came under the censors' knife is an indication that the main impulse of Board decisions does not arise from women's own interests. The Theatres Act acknowledges that there is something to be gained by regulating the amount of pornography available to the public. But like obscenity or other legal strategies that purport to remove materials from the market, the law relies on the more passive action of breaking down barriers to equality rather than the more active advancement of sex equality that comes from giving women a voice in the legal system.

The film community has maintained a consistent stand against censorship, arguing that freedom of expression is as essential to film artists as a camera and projector. Feminist anti-censorship activists added the view that sexuality was high on the feminist agenda, and that as long as that was true, feminists would be exploring this theme in their film art and bearing the burden of film censorship. In response, some anti-pornography feminists have argued that the vulnerability of feminist and progressive film is the price that has to be paid for a policy which greatly diminishes the amount of pornography available to consumers. But the law as it stands doesn't do enough for women. The Film Review Board's eliminations do not in fact remove the sexually subordinating messages of pornography. The law does not recognize the value of sexual equality; it does not compensate the victims; it looks at pictures as if they were images and gives no remedy to women who suffer. It may be true that cutting scenes of extreme sexual violence is useful. But it is obviously a band-aid measure that meets none of the criteria for anti-pornography law, and is plainly not enough to make a significant change in the practice of pornography.

Indeed, none of Canada's existing pornography laws is transformative in ways that can justify the kind of state intervention demanded by pornography law. As we have already seen, a major part of the problem is that Canada's laws have been instituted within a moral framework that misconstrues the meaning of pornography in society in two ways. First, it assumes that the harm of pornography is in the public display of sex, rather than in the use and abuse of women. Second, Canada's Criminal Code strategies, its film censorship policies and its Customs Tariff, interpret pornography as a harmful to society, or as a violation of community standards, not as a violation of women's rights. According to the existing law, when pornographers are punished for breaking the law, they pay their debt to society instead of paying recompense to women. As long as law is constructed to address the abstract idea of morality instead of the concrete realities of women's lives, the law is bound to be ineffective. And as along as Canada's anti-pornography laws fall so short of meeting the seven feminist criteria for a legal strategy against pornography, they cannot be useful and might even cause more harm than good.

5. AN EMPOWERING REMEDY

WOMEN HAVE TRIED to do just about everything they could to fight pornography: they have written letters to law enforcement officers; they have held conferences; they have stood in front of movie theatres protesting the presentation of rape as an erotic spectacle; they have scrawled graffiti on billboards; they have sabotaged men's magazines by placing stickers saying "this exploits women" on the most grisly features; they have complained to the owners of corner stores; they have removed pornography from under their sons' mattresses; they have tried to talk to their husbands; they have asked that the hate literature laws of the Criminal Code be amended to include gender; they have thrown bombs through the windows of stores trafficking in pornography.

Many feminists have struggled with their fury at pornography, their eagerness for the law to take a stand and their fear that legislators and police cannot be trusted. This last concern was intensified when the federal government tabled new amendments to the Criminal Code sections on obscenity under Bill C-54. Even after the Fraser Committee on Pornography and Prostitution had led a thorough national debate on pornography, Bill C-54 wound up only changing the name of the offense from obscenity to pornography, and expanding its definition. Often the problems in the proposed law are there not by design but through sheer sloppiness. Once more, anti-pornography feminists were left to cope with the stupidity of the state machinery.

There are those who think there is a lesson to be learned from the Bill C-54 debacle, and only one solution to the problems of government incompetence and abuse: withdraw from the political debate and oppose any legal action. This perspective presupposes two things. First, it assumes that if those who offer a radical critique of both pornography and government remove themselves from the public discourse, legislators will do likewise. This is unlikely, as the Fraser Report has already become an influential document and the Department of Justice, based on the recommendations of the report, has expressed its determination to make legislative changes. All the polls indicate that the public wants some kind of law. It is naive to suppose that a political culture like Canada's, which has been so comfortable with censorship machinery for years, will suddenly give it up because anti-censorship feminists and civil libertarians want it to. Even if government were to drop Bill C-54, we would still be left with all the existing ineffective and destructive laws.

The second assumption imbedded in the advice to vacate the legislative scene is that every possible legislative strategy has been exhausted. This is not so. All strategies undertaken to combat pornography have either used the Criminal Code as the instrument and/or have invoked the power of law enforcement agents for its implementation. This has led to a choice of two options, both of them repugnant: Do nothing and let the pornography flourish, or do something and wind up stengthening the authority of the misogynist state. What Canadians have not considered is a civil remedy for damages incurred in the practice of pornography.[41] This is a civil remedy for women, not for bureaucracies or the police. A civil remedy allows women to use the legal system to sue pornographers, producers and distributors when women have been injured. These injuries have been described in earlier chapters and by women who have testified in hearings on pornography. They include: forcing women to perform in pornography, forcing women to look at the products of pornography, using pornography as an inspiration for sexual assault, using women in pornography without their consent, and trafficking in the lies that pornography promotes about women, thus impeding women's drive for equality. With such a legal remedy, women could go to court and speak in their own voices about what pornography means to them. If the court agreed that a woman has been injured, and that the materials in question are pornography, then the injured woman could be given relief in the form of monetary damages and/or an injunction against the relevant pornography.

In order to codify a civil remedy, pornography has to be given a legal meaning and a location in law. There are a range of options. Pornography might fit best as a practice of sex discrimination and violation of women's equality under the Charter. Some feminists have begun to draft a Sex Equality Act, legislation something like a Human Rights Code, that establishes the legal principle that women have the right to live free of sexual abuse, and that makes the activities associated with pornography, abuses against prostitutes, and other sexual abuses a violation of the act. Another option is to encode pornography within tort law, which makes a number of personal violations sufficient reason for plaintiffs to seek recourse through the courts. If you trip over a broken stair on somebody's porch, you can sue that person. If a product you have bought explodes and injures you, the tort of product liability gives you the right to sue the manufacturer. Making the practice of pornography a tort — maybe even under product liability itself — names pornography as a legal wrong and allows victims to sue. Giving pornography a place in the Human Rights Code as a violation of women's rights is another option. It is an appealing one, since its enactment would state plainly that pornography violates women's human rights, not society's norms.

Finding the right legal definition of pornography is crucial. Legislators' definitions have consistently failed to describe what pornography actually is. It is not the "undue exploitation of sex" as obscenity law puts it, for if it is, what is "due" exploitation of sex? It is not "any visual material showing vaginal, anal and oral intercourse ... or any other sexual activity" as Bill C-54 puts it, for if that's true, the portrayal of any sexual activity is pornography.

_ What makes pornography different from "any sexual activity" is what it does to women. Pornography subordinates women and it should be defined that way. Echoing the initiatives taken by Andrea Dworkin and Catharine MacKinnon in the Minneapolis Ordinance they wrote, I suggest that pornography is the sexually explicit subordination of women in pictures and/or words that

include one or more of the following:
a. women are presented dehumanized as sexual objects, things or commodities; or
b. women are presented as sexual objects who enjoy humiliation and pain; or
c. women are presented as sexual objects who are being raped or sexually assaulted in any other manner, or who experience sexual pleasure in being raped, or sexually assaulted in any other manner; or
d. women are presented as sexual objects, tied up, cut up, mutilated or bruised or physically hurt; or
e. women are presented in postures or positions of sexual submission, servility or display; or
f. women's body parts — including but not limited to vaginas, breasts or buttocks — are exhibited such that women are reduced to these parts; or
g. women are presented being penetrated by objects or animals; or
h. women are presented in scenarios of degradation, injury, torture, shown as filthy or inferior, bleeding, bruised or hurt in a context that makes these conditions sexual; or
i. women are presented in scenarios of lactation, childbirth or pregnancy in a context that makes these into acts that are understood to be sexually gratifying for another adult; or
k. women, including women who are or who appear to be under the age of eighteen, are presented in scenarios that are described as or suggestive of incest.

Notice the ways in which this legal definition differs from the general definition of pornography used earlier — that pornography is the presentation of sexual subordination for sexual pleasure. But here, precisely because we are looking for a legal definition, the terms are more narrow. First, the materials have to be sexually explicit. This term has a legal meaning, referring either to the presence of penetration or to the explicit display of any genitalia. Second, the definition adds its own list of specific details regarding what the products of pornography have to look like in order to be actionable. These features are there to narrow down the definition. If the words "sexually explicit" were not included, for example, then every subordinating product of culture would be considered pornography. Although it is true that the values and stereotypes of pornography have been mainstreamed by mass media, all those products of mass media are not pornography. And this law is meant to target pornography specifically.

But where this definition meets the one used earlier is in its focus on pornography's main dynamic: sexual subordination. This legal definition makes pornography an action, a specific practice, that includes specific activities: *coercion into pornographic performance, forcing pornography on a person, assault linked to pornography, portraying women in pornography without their consent* and *trafficking in pornography* that stereotypes women and impedes their progress toward equality. With a civil remedy in place, any woman who believes she has been injured by pornography in any of these ways will have the right to state her case in court. It may not be easy, since she will have to complete a number of specific requirements. She must first prove that the relevant materials are pornography. They must be sexually explicit and they must contain one or more of the features listed in the definition. Second, she must prove that the materials sexually subordinated her. The materials have to be more than just offensive; this is not a law that worries about offending sensibilities, it is concerned with injuries to women. These injuries must be proved in court. Only then will the plaintiff be awarded damages or an injunction against the materials in question.

This legal approach is designed to make the pornographer responsible for the sexual subordination in which he trades. If this kind of law were in place in the United States, Linda Marchiano would be able to sue the makers of *Deep Throat* and stop distribution of a film that was made out of her painful experience. In Ontario, the rapist/killer of Barbra Schlifer explained in sworn testimony that he had had a pornographic magazine in his hand when he cut his victim open. With this law, the members of Barbra Schlifer's family could have sued the producer and the distributor of the pornography that was strewn over Schlifer's body. Any woman whose picture is published against her will as pornography would have a case against the producers and the traffickers of the pornography. In the U.S., former Miss America Vanessa Williams would have been able to sue *Penthouse* publisher Bob Guccione for fraudulent induction into pornography. Any woman forced to look at pornography while paying her bill at a variety store would have a similar case against the proprietor. And the hundreds of women who are forced to replicate the sexual acts in pornography would finally be empowered to sue pornography traffickers for the violation they have experienced. They can still charge their rapists with sexual assault, or their batterers with assault. But they have an additional legal tool to use against the pornographers who promote the sexual violence women experience.

But what about radical artists? Why should they have to worry about the ways in which their sexual explorations are contextualized? Searchers for alternative erotica worry that they might have to pay a penalty because pornography has created a sexual crisis that distorts the meaning of sexual art and turns educational materials into weapons for subordination, even if no subordination was intended. What would happen if an artist with the best intentions discovered that her work was used to hurt someone? A well-meaning feminist could publish a series of women's violent sexual fantasies with the stated purpose of illustrating how sexually colonized women are. But what if a woman were forced by her partner to engage in the activities?

Artists use the word empowerment to describe the process of their making an imprint on the world with their art. What this remedy does is ask that artists consider the meaning of the word empowerment. Most see it only in positive terms. I act, therefore I am empowered. I draw, therefore I am empowered to envision. I produce sexually explicit materials, and therefore I am empowered to make change. And all this must be to the good. Why? What if art has a negative impact? It is possible that our feminist chronicler of sexual fantasy winds up with a lawsuit. What then? Having heard this question repeatedly, I am consistently troubled by the fact that so much caring can go out to the artist while so little goes to the woman who was forced into sex. It seems to me that the soon-to-be-wronged creator has to go to the already wronged victim and talk this through. That strikes me as empowerment — to take what you know, what you meant, and deal with it with someone who has been hurt by something that you did.

Many anti-censorship activists have opposed this approach, claiming that it is almost too democratic: it gives right-wing women the right to harass the distributors of radical sexual art and same-sex materials. The trafficking provision, historically the most contentious element of the civil remedy, says that the very act of distributing pornography is a harm to women. The opponents of censorship contend that this aspect of the remedy is not concrete. Nor is it based on specific actions like coercion, assault or force. What would happen if the wrong people used the remedy against the wrong materials? The answer is that such a law would not allow people to go to court with a claim that materials do not suit them, or do not fit into their value system. Here is where the trafficking provision proves to be quite concrete: claimants must show categorically that the materials subordinated them, made them less than human, or lowered them in the social system. A right-winger who thinks pornography is anti-family cannot use this remedy, for there is nothing subordinating about advocating recreational sex. Immoral it may be, according to conservative doctrine, but subordinating it is not. The judge should reject such a claim. On the other hand, if the so-called radical sexual art does negate women or objectify them, and a right-wing woman can show with evidence how this has injured her, she can make her case. Human rights, after all, were never conceived only for those who have progressive politics.

Other critics of this legal strategy, especially in the United States, charge that a civil remedy treats women as victims. For instance, prostitutes' rights groups have opposed civil suits against pornography, arguing that they stereotype prostitutes as victims in pornography. It is almost unbelievable that an organization representing prostitutes, just because it believes prostitution per se is not an abuse, would actually oppose a prostitute's right to seek damages when she has been hurt. After all, if she has not been hurt, she would not have a case and would not file suit.

The claim that feminism sees women only as victims has dogged women's rights activists throughout the second wave of the women's movement. Yet it's difficult to figure out how a feminist can talk about sexism without describing its abusive practices; and it's impossible to fathom a way to change women's subordinate status unless we can show how it is acted out in real life. Certainly with this law, women will be heard describing their pain in court. There they will have the chance to challenge pornographers, which is the opposite of making women victims.

The civil remedy for pornography grows out of an awareness of what pornography is and does. Its commitment to the idea that pornography is a practice is evident from its strategy of making specific activities — coercion, force, assault, portrayal without consent and trafficking — actionable. The law focusses on the pictures, words or ideas only when it comes time to determine whether the actionable materials are bona fide pornographs. The materials in question must be sexually explicit and they must contain one or more of the features listed in the definition. These features were developed by looking at the products of pornography and describing them. And they are included so that the law will target pornographs specifically, and not the full range of sexist media products.

This law was conceived expressly with the understanding that what happens to women in the production and consumption phases of pornography matters. It arose out of testimony offered by women about the ways in which they were forced into pornography so that pornography could be forced on other women. At hearings held in Minneapolis to validate the Minneapolis Ordinance, hundreds of women testified that pornography was used to train and humiliate them and to make them feel less than human.[42]

Because the law takes women into account, it insists on cutting through the public/private split nurtured in other laws and which has protected many of the perpetrators of male violence. Existing obscenity law targets the distributors of pornography; possession in private is not covered by the law. The Theatres Acts exist to regulate the public exhibition of film; private production and viewing is not covered by the law. Up to now, what goes on in public is subject to regulation and what goes on in the home is beyond the law's scope. This civil remedy takes into account the fact that a great deal of the violence women exerience goes on in private. This law does not make *possession* in private actionable, but it does make the assaults that are incurred privately in the practice of pornography vulnerable to a suit.

The language of the civil remedy proposed here is decidedly gender-specific, defining pornography as the sexually explicit subordination of women. But this gender specificity is such that it can still make room for men, children and transsexuals to file suits. The original Minneapolis Ordinance was drafted to include these groups. But they can use the law only when they are treated the way women are treated in pornography. For example, if a man has been coerced into pornography, he can file suit against the producers. By drafting the law in this way, the gender-specificity of pornography is recognized, and no one can get the impression that the practice is gender-neutral. But at the same time the strategy gives all people access to the law if they have been hurt.

When the state used law in the past, it harnessed the agents of law enforcement, encouraging men in blue to sweep in and to exercise all the authority they can muster. Often they have used military tactics, and usually theirs is the last word before trial. This aspect of state authority and its dynamic of dominance is patriarchal to the core. As experience goes, there is not that much difference between the bullying actions of the police and the bullying actions of assaultive husbands. Whether the authority comes from the state or male privilege, male power over women and the control of the state over the public are both dominance. The civil remedy for pornography was conceived for precisely this reason. It is not a criminal law. It provides for no new power for the police and instead empowers women, who are best situated to know the harm of pornography. The law makes women visible and gives them the voice they never had in the legal system.

Civil remedies do, however, require that the plaintiff foot the legal bills for her suit. This is potentially a problem since many women do not have the money for these expensive legal battles. This is especially true of those women who were in positions to be abused in the making of pornography — they were poor and needed the money in the first place. It is possible, though, that the plantiffs could get some financial assistance from women's organizations. For example, if pornography were legally defined in sex equality law, then the Legal Education and Action Fund (LEAF), which was established to help women make Charter challenges, might be able to help. It may be, though, that women will have to raise funds on their own. In any case, already there are lawyers interested in the anti-pornography strategy of using civil remedies, who may agree to work for smaller fees.

Civil remedies exist to give relief for the victims. This civil remedy for pornography makes it possible for women who are hurt to seek and receive damages — actual funds — for the harms they experience. Awarding damages to women makes the trafficking of pornography — including the manufacturing and distributing — a financial risk instead of sure-fire moneymaker. No trafficker could be sure that the pornographs he is moving across the country will not be used against women in situations of force. Most professions that put the practitioner at risk are highly paid. Since pornography is already a high-paying business, it makes sense to infuse it with the kind of risk that matches its financial rewards. Perhaps this law will dissuade pornographers from going into the business of subordinating women for profit. The idea is to make pornographers wonder, to make them aware that women will fight back if they are abused by pornographic practices, and to make sure that it is the pornographer who pays. This is a vast improvement over taking fines and putting them into government accounts, as if pornography harmed the government and not women.

Especially if the law is drafted in the context of Canada's Charter of Rights and Freedoms, and makes pornography a form of sex discrimination, the law will advance women's equality interests. But even if the law is put together as something other than a violation of women's human rights, the dynamic of the civil remedy — especially its implementation — would operate in a way that would transform gender inequality. The law gives women the kind of voice they have never had in the context of anti-pornography law. It allows women to say, "I have been hurt," and gives these women access to the courts to describe what has happened to them. Women's silence has been enforced by the shame, fear, humiliation and force of sexual abuse, but a civil remedy breaks down that silence, giving new meaning to the often abused term "freedom of speech."

Pornography helps to maintain women's second-class status by exploiting the most financially vulnerable and by making women appear to be good for sex only, and for no other work. Thus it is fitting that the law provides women with financial compensation for the harms they have experienced. While pornography institutionalizes women's financial inequality, this law seeks to remedy the situation by offering women the chance for some kind of financial reward.

Sexual explicitness per se is not actionable under this law. This means that sex education materials are not vulnerable and neither are truly alternative artistic explorations of eroticism. Artists who use subordinating materials as examples of women's oppression are not vulnerable to the law, for their practice obviously does not subordinate women. This does not mean, however, that everything artistic, or everything exhibited in art galleries, cannot be implicated in this legal process. This law does not place art above women's lives. When sexually explicit materials, even if expressed with the most impressive virtuosity, subordinate women, calling the producer an artist would not place him out of the reach of the law.

Unlike Canada's existing anti-pornography laws, there is nothing in the civil remedy that targets lesbian and gay sexual materials. But for the sake of clarity, the law could be drafted with a special section stating explicitly that gay and lesbian materials are not pornography by definition. However, the law cannot protect lesbian and gay materials that are subordinating. If they subordinate women, they will be just as vulnerable to the law as heterosexual materials.

To be sure, the law relies to a great extent on the existing male-dominated legal structures. But the increased consciousness of judges evidenced in the changing face of obscenity law is a sign that the courts can learn, however slowly, what is subordinating and what is not, that they are keeping an eye on the discourse and can be influenced by feminist ideas. Almost all, the recent decisions on pornography law show judges leaning away from judgements that hurt artistic, sex education and same-sex materials. This new awareness can be applied to the administration of a civil remedy. Then again, right-wingers cannot just sweep onto the scene, laying complaints against materials that offend them or run counter to their values. There is only one standard embedded in this law: a strong stand against sexually explicit materials that subordinate women.

This legal strategy poses no threat to the development of alternative erotica; it does not make sex education materials subject to prosecution; it gives victimized women the financial support they need; it allows women who are dehumanized in the making and consuming of pornographs to reclaim some humanity through court action.

A civil remedy will not eliminate pornography or end violence against women. But no law on its own has ever had such miraculous powers. Good law is accompanied by education and activism that promote the values instituted by the legal strategy. That part of the feminist project has to continue. But in the meantime, a law that insists that when a woman is hurt she should be able to do something about it, a law that states clearly that women matter, is a vast improvement over Canada's bloated and ineffective censorship machinery.

CHAPTER III

THE SEX CRISIS

1

WHEN I BEGAN TO SPEAK PUBLICLY ABOUT PORNOGRAPHY I was often faced with the charge that I was anti-sex. American opposition to anti-pornography initiatives has been vociferous in this claim, and new books by so-called pro-sex forces, some of them by women calling themselves feminist, have continued to argue that fighting pornography is the same as waging war against human sexuality. I fought against the charge, convinced in the first place that my subject was pornography and not sex at all. When I finally recognized that I had to face the reality I myself had uncovered, namely that the sexual subordination of pornography exists for sexual pleasure, I still would not accept the anti-sex label.

I thought instead that sexuality was unremittingly positive and life-affirming, that pornography distorted this very essence of sex[1] and that these and other forces vied with each for control over our bodies. I imagined that even with these forces competing for influence, sex was subjective, and that every person played out her or his identity in the sexual arena with all of the diversity that exists within the human race. None of these ideas changed the minds of those people who were sure I was on a campaign against sexual pleasure.

Now I understand that I am against sexual pleasure *as pornography and mass culture construct it*. I no longer believe that the words "sexuality" and "diversity" must be uttered in the same breath. I differ with those who defend sexuality no matter what its content and who believe we have free choice in sex. I think instead that there is really one narrow definition of sexuality in our culture and the sexual choices so many people wish we had are illusory. They are as illusory as our "choice" of 25 brands of toothpaste, all of which contain the same ingredients, or our choice of politicians, who with the exception of a few platform planks, still govern in more or less the same way.

The emergence of a booming industry, with its specific formula for sexual gratification, suggests that what sparks sexual pleasure is not just one spectacular coincidence. Pornographers create and reinforce the substance of sexual pleasure, distributing what they know will turn on their consumers. They make unhindered access to women sexy, hierarchy sexy, rape sexy, violence sexy, women getting hurt sexy. And it "works." They do not have to wrack their brains to figure out how to flick sexual switches, because through their promotion of a specific sexual construct, they have already defined what will work. Thus, pornography and its messages do not constitute one of many ideologies competing at random in a free market for social and sexual dominance. And certainly, the sexuality we experience is not a product of nature. Rather, pornography actively constructs and narrows our sexual choices.

The sexual values of female victimization and male conquest are not just located in pornography. Let's return to our imaginary scenario in which a man and a woman are arguing and the decibel level of their voices rises. She brushes past him to leave, and he grabs her by the arm and pulls her to him so that they are almost nose to nose. Imagine it. Almost everyone watching would think these two are about to have hot sex.

Why? What makes violence and conflict so sexually appealing? Why is power such a turn-on? The fact is that this woman may or may not be about to have sex, but what is certain is that she is going to have bruises on her arm. Why do sex and female hurt go together? I think it's because sexual pleasure is not, after all, a random thing, but is closely constructed in terms of male power and female powerlessness. In pornography's rape scenarios, women wind up on their backs suffering for their orgasms. In violent scenarios, it is usually the woman who gets hurt. Think about the steamy sex sequences in movies that have moved so many people. Rhett Butler attacks Scarlett O'Hara on the stairs of their home (*Gone With the Wind*); a drifter and the wife of a gas station/cafe owner sexually collide on the kitchen table while knives clatter ominously onto the floor (*The Postman Always Rings Twice*); Maddie and Dave finally have sex after years of flirtation on prime time, but they have to slap each other around for foreplay (*Moonlighting*). This is called romance. Is there no pattern here? In whose interests is it that sexual desire and pleasure be constructed this way?

Perhaps apologists for pornography who feared that fighting pornography's influence was tantamount to battling against sex itself have a point. They are convinced that if pornography disappeared they would never have sex again. Deep down, they understand something fundamental: a struggle against pornography is a struggle against existing sexual norms and a battle to redefine the terms for sexual pleasure. If pornography constructs the way so many people feel sexual pleasure, if pornography's market is burgeoning and its influence growing, then sexuality itself does have to come under close scrutiny. And if pornography constructs scenarios of male sexual power and female sexual powerlessness, then pornography is political, playing an important role in constructing the dominant sexual ideology of female subordination. Pornography is political and yes, so is sex.

Sex is political. This statement will astonish many people who believe, as I did, that sexuality is the last bastion of individualism, the only remaining frontier on which people can indulge their personal tastes and desires. Bring up the subject of sexual likes and dislikes and you can count on the quick observation that "everyone is different." Suggest that sexual response and desire are socially constructed to correspond to the gender hierarchy of power and dominance, and someone is bound to reply in something of a panic that it doesn't work that way, and that everyone is sexually free.

I sympathize with the view, for I held it myself at one time. No one likes to believe that they are being manipulated or victimized (consider some women's resistance to feminism!), especially about something that has been mythologized as being part of personal identity. But I do find it peculiar when these notions are expressed by observers with radical analyses on almost every other subject. Anti-censorship activists insist that the state and its laws are constructed to be used by the powerful against the powerless. They might allow that one judge can be more progressive than the other, but they would never dispense with their overall analysis of the law by saying it depends on who's on the bench that day. Socialists say that work and the means of production are organized to use workers to make profits for capitalists. They would not say that it depends on who owns the factory. Feminists will say that patriarchal structures such as the church and the family exist to maintain the sexist status quo of male dominance and rigid sex roles. They would not say that it depends on who you marry.

But samples of the writings from all of these groups, including some feminists, reveal a weird collective cave-in when the subject turns to sex.[2] Suddenly the sentiment that diversity reigns in the sexual arena takes over. Suddenly sexuality is the ultimate individual expression. Left-leaning entertainment weeklies refuse ads for the Ku Klux Klan but have no problem publishing personal ads from white readers looking for black sexual slaves. The ads for the Ku Klux Klan are ads for racism, but the ads for black sex slaves are, well, for sex, and for the individual's right to choose his or her pleasure — as if it is a coincidence that anyone would "choose" to eroticize racism.[3] These attitudes create the ideas behind what I call sex liberalism. It is an appealing ideology that blinds us to the real workings of sex in our society.

The idea of free choice in sexuality is a liberal fiction feminists have to expose and then bury. If the forces of political dominance have been so rigorous and so careful to appropriate every other avenue of expression and social change, why and how can we imagine that they would have left sexuality out? In fact, the products of culture that I mentioned just above are propaganda that creates the sexual ideology of forced sex, male dominance and female submission. The work of this propaganda is very influential. It not only reflects the real world, it creates it, combining with other factors and experiences — such as objectification, sex manuals and especially sexual abuse — to create a sexual ideology deeply rooted in the dynamics of sexual subordination. This ideology has profound effects on what makes us feel good.[4]

It shapes our sexual world. It promotes sexual subordination as the key to sexual desire. It creates the links in a chain that binds women and men to — not just sex roles — but *sexual* roles that replicate and reinforce social conditions of male power and female powerlessness. What holds the links together is the basic sex dynamic that fuses the sexual meaning of male with dominance and the sexual meaning of female with submission. This dynamic is tied into the first link of the chain: the social process of sex-role stereotyping and the strategies through which young children are streamed into sex roles quickly and effectively. The process often starts at birth. In teaching hospitals nurses still will not give blankets to new mothers until they know the gender of the baby, so that the babies will get the right colour blanket: girls pink, boys blue. In hospital nurseries, bassinets are plastered with heavily-pencilled signs saying "it's a boy" or "it's a girl," presumably to subvert gender confusion. What can possibly confuse a two-hour old is not exactly clear. Even banks gender their bankbooks for baby's new bank account: pink for girls, blue for boys. Girls are thus inducted into an intense process of "pinkification" while boys are forever "blued," and the colour codes translate into intensely streamed sex roles.

These sex roles slide into sexual roles when women and men start having to conform to their gendered wardrobes. Dress codes set the terms and forge a second link in the imprisoning shackles of dominance and submission. Consider what women are expected to wear: High-heeled shoes create the teetering effect, skirts, especially tight ones, make a purposeful stride impossible, garters (currently making a fashion comeback to compete with the much more comfortable panty hose) cut into thighs, tight sweaters promote torso jiggle. While many women believe their wardrobes allow them to make individual fashion statements, again the choices are illusory. What is really going on is that they choose from women's dresses designed to make them appear available and to hinder their mobility at the same time. On the other hand, men wear pants and flat shoes without much worry about restricted movements. They don't have to. They aren't threatened by sexual assault in the same way women are. Yet the female dress codes makes it impossible for women to defend themselves against the physical or sexual assault that is a real threat for them.

The painful irony of all of this is that all the hours spent on cosmetic application and the dollars spent on clothes usually are mustered for the express purpose of making women sexually appealing. What does that say about what sex is supposed to be and how the participants are expected to behave? Women: inanimate, available, submissive. Men: mobile, active, dominant. The language of sexuality reflects the dominant/submissive paradigm. Men take, women are taken. Women surrender, men conquer. And so viewers often do not see that when Rhett Butler sweeps the protesting Scarlett O'Hara up in his arms, that is not romance, it is rape. There are thousands of women who read Harlequin romances for rivetting accounts of the challenge of the tall dark stranger's steely glare. These avid readers may agree that the hero's cruel gaze is the expression of the essence of male sexuality. But they do not see that the fluttering heart of the heroine is a heart consigned to a life of submission through sex, and that through this sexual dynamic, male and female sexuality are defined in a way that maintains the social order.

Penthouse publisher Bob Guccione argues that women are natural exhibitionists so that he can rationalize the exploitation of women in his magazine. But women do not take off their clothes by nature, or else why would they take money for it? Women do not turn themselves into sexual objects; rather, the pressures to conform to gender expectations enforce their roles as objects. So do pornographers, and so do advertisers who promote products while sexually objectifying women. All of these cultural phenomena limit how women perceive and present themselves. They also limit how men want to see women. Over the centuries, the constant display and objectification of women's bodies has made it seem that it is men's natural privilege to leer at women.[5]

This institutionalized objectification reinforces another link in the sexual ideology of male dominance and female submission. The male gaze becomes an active position of dominance, while the female object of the look takes on the passive role of submission.[6] These stances become inextricably bound up in the definitions of male and female per se. A women who does not wear cosmetics, or long hair as an ornament, or make-up or clothes that display her body, learns that these social expectations define how she will be perceived, for often she will be mistaken for a man. She learns that being female means taking the time to pre-pare to be looked at. No wonder *Viva*, the magazine that encouraged women to look at nude men, failed so miserably. Men could not suddenly be transformed into sex objects and women could not take up the dominant position of looking without undermining the strict codes of male dominance and female submission.

Cultural representation does a great deal to make the paradigm of male dominance and female submission seem natural instead of socially constructed. So successful is the strategy that the dominance/submission pattern has been rendered almost invisible. In addition, the dominance/submission pattern is so prevalent that when it *is* visible, it is made to look absolutely reasonable, even in the face of its own illogic. Consider the narrative in Lina Wertmuller's film *Swept Away*. A ruling-class woman is lounging on her yacht, attended by her working-class houseboy, when a storm sweeps them both away to a deserted island. There the power relations of class are radically transform-ed into the power of men over women.

Eventually the houseboy rapes his female boss. Most of the controversy aroused by the film centred on its presentation of the classic rape myth. But there was a second component to the se-quence that was more fascinating. He says to her while he is assaulting her: "I am doing this to you because of what you did to me." She had teased him mercilessly, writhing around in a skimpy bikini when she knew he was looking at her, and she ob-viously had enjoyed the power she gained from her complete in-accessibility. And so he says to her, "You did this to me and so I am doing this to you." An eye for an eye but no, this is no fair ex-change. An equal exchange would have him writhing on the sand in a skimpy bikini, not letting her near him. He rapes her instead. She teases, he rapes. The ways these sexual antagonists expressed sexual power were completely different. In the context, it was barely noticed by viewers that a rape for a tease is an exchange of opposites, not of likes. Yet his rape of her is utterly sensible within the paradigm of male dominance and female submission, so sensible that he can argue that it constitutes real sexual equali-ty and the filmgoers would agree.

This warped eye-for-an-eye view has its counterpart in real life. Certainly young men are infuriated when women have the gall to arouse them and not follow through, as if a stiff penis were something other than a muscle filling with blood. Why does an erection unsatisfied so often translate into male anger? Why is it so easy for people to say that if a woman gets a man aroused, she deserves to be raped? The fact is that in the history of mankind, no one has ever died of an erection.

Another link in the dominant sexual ideology's chain is created by pressure on women to marry and conform to the traditional nuclear family's requirement that she meet the sexual demands of her husband. Until 1983, spousal rape did not exist within law, thus establishing husbands' unlimited access to their wives. Even with the changes in sexual assault law, a marriage can still be annulled if sexual intercourse has not taken place, which in itself is a strong indication that sex is meant to be part of the marriage package deal. Many women secretly harbour the knowledge that in order to maintain their marriages — and personal respectability and legitimacy in their communities — they will have to spread their legs regularly. This is especially true of women who have never considered an alternative to marriage and who were reared in a social system where if you were not affixed to a man, you were a failure as a woman.

Although to a certain extent options have opened up for women, especially in urban centres, there are still many women who do not feel complete unless they have a male partner. Some women's identities are so bound up in their emotional relationships that they cannot even see themselves out of them. This happens to many assaulted women but it happens as well in marriages where the abuse is not overt. In traditional relationships, where the roles are especially rigid, women have been expected to be selfless and nurturing in their emotional lives, and they are encouraged to be the same way in bed. They do not necessarily experience this as rape, but they wind up having to settle for meeting their partner's needs by making themselves available for sexual use. Their desperation is sealed in the knowledge that sex is part of the marital package deal and that if they don't deliver, they may be discarded for someone else who will. So they are willing to do almost anything to keep their sexual partners. This is how sexuality negates women. This is how sex itself becomes a deeply coercive activity, something women do to survive, to maintain what they think is their identity.

Sex manuals often masquerade as sex-education materials,[7] pushing women into sex they do not want to have by encouraging them to meet men's sexual demands at all costs. Alexandra Penney's book *Great Sex*[8] offers a splendid example of the syndrome. Her tips on fellatio technique make it clear whose pleasure counts. "Oral sex is important to men for several reasons," she advises. "The first is that it just plain feels great. And second, oral sex confirms that a woman enjoys that part of a man's body that is most important to him." Penney is well-schooled in the prevailing sexual ideology: what feels good to men is the most important thing, and she is absolutely convinced that the penis is the centre of the sexual universe. She tells women that the part which is most important to men should also be most important to women too.

"Relax, remember to breathe," counsels the sex therapist. Women's physical and emotional discomfort with this activity is completely discounted. "If you're having any mental problems with what you're doing, concentrate completely on your physical actions." A well-sucked penis is much more important than whatever physical discomfort may go with it. Penney delivers her advice on the matter in terms that are completely male-centred:

> If your man likes to put as much of his penis into your mouth as he can, you may prefer to stick with saliva as a lubricant, unless he prefers something else. If he wants to thrust while in your mouth, you may have a tendency to gag. If it happens, don't be upset. Take a second's pause, a deep breath to relax your throat muscles, and keep on going.

Everything — the lubricant, the depth of the sucking, the extent of the penile thrust — depends on what the man wants. Never once does Penney allow that trauma and lovemaking do not go together. Never once does she suggest a choking reaction to anything is a good enough reason to stop. Keep on going, she exhorts. She does not even consider that a sensitive and caring male might want his partner to stop if she is uncomfortable. The men who exist in Penney's sexual universe make non-negotiable sexual demands of their female partners and could not care less how they react. Penney's material is propaganda for sexual abuse.

Women's experience with sexual abuse does much to construct the female sexuality of submission. According to an extraordinary study undertaken by Ayala Pines, Mimi Silbert and the women of Delancey House in California, 66 per cent of the juvenile prostitutes surveyed revealed that incest was a part of their personal biographies. Having fled homes where the abuse occurred, thse women carry with them a great deal of emotional baggage. The ongoing abuse they experienced at home makes them tolerant of abusive relationships, especially those with pimps, and creates a situation where it is extremely difficult for them to make sense of early abuses. Explaining the syndrome, Pines and Silbert describe how these women react "with depression, inaction and self blame." As the abuses continue, "the women retreat into a totally passive role in which they feel powerless, out of control of their lives, debilitated and psychologically paralyzed."[9]

Clinical studies of incest survivors report that few of them breeze through life without any fallout from the experience.[10] Many report having difficulty with sex, not trusting their orgasms, worrying that their sexual pleasure does not come from a good place. Still, most believe that they were the ones who had done something wrong, that they should be punished, and that if no one will mete out justice, they will administer it to themselves. Many of them survive rape later on, because as Pines and Silbert remark, their subject group had developed a tendency not to be able to recognize when they are in dangerous situations. Revictimization has been uncovered in other areas of violence against women as well. Diana Russell reveals that a disproportionate number of rape victims were incest survivors.[11] Shelter workers report with deep distress that many women pull them themselves together to leave one assaultive relationship only to move onto another one.

These situations have been interpreted as proof of women's natural masochism, but there is nothing natural about these events.[12] The prevalence of sexual assault in society has a profound effect on women's sexuality, constructing women's sexual and emotional responses into the sexuality of subordination. Women with sexual abuse in their biographies have described how the experience taught them how to make victimization feel pleasurable. Many incest survivors despairingly report having orgasms in sexual situations they do not control. Their sexuality has been moulded to fit within the frame of powerlessness so that they continue to respond sexually in conditions of force. Young prostitutes who have survived incest have learned from their first sexual experiences that sex takes place within a context of their own vulnerability, at the hands of men whose authority over them is total. Being owned, especially for sex, becomes a continuation of a pattern established by prior events. Prostitution becomes an experience of the universe unfolding as it always has. If a woman has never really owned her own body, selling it will not feel much like a violation. If she has had her sexuality stolen from her practically all her life, then getting money for sex seems like an empowering alternative, increasing her mobility and control. And nights with a controlling pimp, someone nearer her own age, someone who promises money and clothes, at least in the first stages of the relationship, would seem heavenly compared to those endless nights at home waiting for the inevitable turn of the bedroom doorknob.

Many wife assault victims suffer spousal rape, feeling nothing sexually, but some reluctantly admit that the sex does turn them on. They confuse their husband's controlling behaviour with love, automatically responding to their husband's violent sexuality with sexual surrender that does feel good to them. Not surprisingly, many of these women are the ones who leave one assaultive man only to take up with another one. This is how women act out abuse through the erotic system of male dominance and female submission. Cultural products and socialized sexual roles are not the only things that keep women in line with the prevailing sexual ideology. Real experience works just as well.

Male experience is very little like female experience, except — and this is a notable exception — during childhood, when males are as vulnerable to sexual assault as females. It is true that girls are assaulted many more times than boys, but boys' vulnerability and powerlessnes vis-a-vis their abusers represents one of the few instances of lived sexual equality. But consider what happens to male and female survivors. The research shows that many female survivors learn from the experience to tolerate abuse and thus, especially if there has been no counselling intervention, become revictimized later in life. The male victims, however, go on to become sexual abusers thmeselves.[13] Between childhood and adulthood a dramatic shift takes place, shaping two opposing behaviours out of the same experience. Boy victims become victimizers, girl victims continue to be victims, sure proof of the ideological force of male dominance and female submission.

Of course not all sexual abusers have been victimized themselves. The prevailing sexual ideology of female subordination is powerful enough on its own. Its ascendency may help explain why children are so sexually appealing to so many men and why youthful sexuality has always been so desirable. A passive, helpless, vulnerable (almost always female) victim fits well into the dominant ideology. In fact, we could go so far as to say that rape itself would not be so prevalent were sex not tied so closely to the dominance/submission pattern. If all of this sounds like a reversal of the long-held feminist view that rape is about power and not sex, it is just that: a reconsideration of feminist views on sexual assault.

I suspect that feminist activists retreated into the "rape is about power" stance, making sure they never confused sex with rape, so that they could in effect salvage sex in a patriarchal system — as if wishful thinking can salvage anything. As well, some legal observers who were aware that many rapists use weapons other than the penis felt that a law that defined rape as penile penetration left out the assaults perpetrated with, say, pop bottles or broomsticks. That the penis is not the weapon in the assault does not mean that sex is not involved: saying rape is about power and not sex leaves out the crucial fact of where the attackers put their weapons. If rape is about power and not sex, why don't attackers just hit women, and exercise their power that way?[14] Because *rape is sex to them.* Pornography has played a key role in creating this dynamic. As we have seen, rape myths that present women getting sexual pleasure from rape have been very successful in convincing viewers that women really like force in sex.

Male predators know how to find women who have been so completely cowed that they cannot resist them. Wife beaters know who is vulnerable. They can tell by a woman's reactions to situations, by her inability to defend herself. Sexual harassers make a point of choosing women who are isolated, who apparently have no friends and who will have no one to talk to if they think they're being victimized. Although women's previous trauma in sex works to target them, sometimes a victim's lack of sexual experience makes her vulnerable and unable to negotiate her way through the sexual encounter with a harasser. In the streets, a pimp hits up on the girls he knows he can control. If a woman shows signs of self-worth and an ability to protect herself, he will move on and find someone he *can* control.

A recent survey undertaken in a suburb of Toronto reports that people are conforming to dominance and submission patterns at an early age. One out of seven male students in grade thirteen reports already having refused to take no for an answer, and one out of four females reported having been forced in a sexual situation.[15] These percentages are taken out of the entire grade thirteen class, not just from among those students who were sexually active. In spite of hopes to the contrary, pornography and mass culture are working to collapse sexuality with rape, reinforcing the patterns of male dominance and female submission so that many young people believe that this is simply the way sex is. This means that many of the rapists of the future will believe that they are behaving within socially accepted norms.

Another link in the chain of the dominant sexual ideology ties sexuality to the dynamics of violence, tension and conflict. Any woman (or man for that matter) who has ever been given the finger, that hostile digital salute, knows where the finger is supposed to go, and has to wonder how that sexual act became imbued with so much hatred. Descriptions of sexual exchanges, whether pornographic or otherwise, smoulder with the rhetoric forged by this link in the ideology. Phrases such as "sexual tension," "love-hate relationships," "pain equals pleasure" and others reinforce the dynamic. The word "violence" may be gender-neutral but the experience is not. Its gendered component lies in the decided physical edge that men have in most violent encounters with women. A male/female slugfest is far more likely to produce a female rather than a male victim, and this is just as true if the conflict is consummated by sex. The ideological force given to violence in sex constructs sexual encounters in which women emerge bloodied, yet pleasured.

Earlier we discussed the ease with which we tend to confuse a hot sexual encounter with a circumstances that are violent and hurtful to women. Pornography research has illustrated how likely it is that this will happen. When Ed Donnerstein began his research program, he wanted to devise his own sexually explicit materials for use in the laboratory. At one point, he was attempting to develop materials that featured men and women in violent but non-sexual scenarios so that he could compare their impact with materials that featured explicit sexually violent scenes. He discovered that every time he presented violent encounters between a man and a woman, a significant percentage of his subjects perceived them as sexual.[16] No matter how hard Donnerstein tried to remove any sexual content — everyone's clothes are on, there is no genital contact, no kissing, no jiggling — his subjects still saw sex in male/female violence. If they did not see sex per se, they saw foreplay. The dominant sexual ideology is strong enough to merge sexuality with violence no matter the attempts to desexualize conflict.

The impact of the propaganda is powerful and disturbing. On a music program telecast on Toronto's CITY TV, four barely post-pubescent fans of the heavy metal band Motley Crue were interviewed by Daniel Richler. Heavy metal — guys and guitars — is a genre of pop music committed to head-banging and a sexual stance that exudes violence. Far from being an extreme phenomenon, heavy metal constitutes the top-selling rock genre in both Canada and the United States. Of the top ten albums sold in Canada in 1987, six were a part of the heavy metal genre. Though religious rightists think rock and roll is the devil's gift, satan is not a player here, male power is. On this particular magazine item, one fourteen-year-old girl was asked what she thought of Motley Crue's violence-saturated videos, which portray women as sexual slaves in cages. In an ideologically revealing moment, she referred to the lead singer in the band and said, "Tommy Lee can hurt me any time he wants."

Chances are this girl does not know what it would feel like to be beaten up by Tommy Lee or anybody else. Probably if she had her choice between being beaten up or treated kindly by the singer she would choose the latter. What she really wants is for Tommy Lee to be a completely different person. But since being with Lee would give her a certain amount of status, she is prepared to accept that being roughed up a bit might be part of the package. How desperate is she for status? Enough so that she will do anything to keep any male partner? What will happen when she starts having sex with her boyfriend and he wants it heavy metal style? Will she say no, this does not feel good for me, or will she decide that since this is what sex is, then she is going to have to get used to it? The study undertaken in the Toronto suburb confirms the worst case scenario. Some 80 per cent of the girls reported they were already involved in violent relationships. Most of them said that fear of losing these relationships prevented them from protesting in violent situations. These young women, and the young men who reported having already forced girls into sex, make it painfully clear that we are in the middle of a deeply-rooted sexual crisis.

Adding to the crisis is another link in the chain of the dominant/submissive ideology, the cultural definition of sex as sexual intercourse only. A female who has had sexual intercourse for the first time is said to have "become a woman," as if this were the only way she could define her identity. The term foreplay refers to just about every sexual activity other than sexual intercourse, denoting the extraordinary emphasis we give to one particular practice. People wonder what lesbians do. Legislatures enact homophobic laws against sexual practices that do not conform to this link in the ideology. What Adrienne Rich called compulsory heterosexuality[17] — and its legal structure of laws and ordinances that deny gay rights — is an oppressive byproduct of society's insistence that there is only one suitable sexual practice.

Perhaps the best evidence of the dominance/submissive pattern within the institution of sexual intercourse is the language used to describe it in pornography and everyday life. When not reduced by the animal imagery of beaver or pussy, itself a subordinating factor, women's genitals are gashes, slits, cunts and twats, while the penis — lance, prick, etc. — is made to sound more like a weapon than anything else. Through sexual intercourse, women are pumped, porked, put, ploughed, screwed, but mostly fucked. It is no coincidence that the word fuck is used as often to describe someone destroying or doing damage to someone else as it is to describe sex.

In non-explicit mainstream pornography women are presented as holes to be plugged by consumers. In sexually explicit pornography, although fellatio is decidedly a preoccupation, it is still portrayed as foreplay to the main event: sexual intercourse presented through intense closeups of the penetration. Gay male sex is invisible, except in materials aimed specifically at the gay male market. Lesbianism, on the other hand, has a hefty profile. Either lesbian sex is offered as something for men to look at and thus control, or lesbianism is used to help identify the female villain in the scenario (she is usually a Sapphic predator). But most of the time, lesbian sex is portrayed as an encounter between women that is interrupted by a man who can show them the "real thing."

We see this ideological bind presented by sexual intercourse when heterosexual women cannot figure out how to "have sex" without getting pregnant. Walking into a birth control clinic can be downright depressing. The tables are cluttered with pamphlets that painstakingly describe the available methods of birth control. None of them has a 100 per cent success rate and the one with the highest success rate, the birth control pill, has so many attendant risks that it becomes a less than a desirable choice. Since women are discouraged from taking the pill for longer than five years, any woman who is heterosexually active from her late teens through her adult life will wind up with at least one other contraceptive option. She can choose to insert an intrauterine device, a copper foreign object with plenty of toxic potential, into her uterus; use a diaphragm, which cannot promise better than a 90 per cent success rate; or opt for a condom, which in the days of AIDS is becoming more popular but which has always been the nemesis of sexual spontaneity and whose failure rate is even higher than the diaphragm's. Much personal anguish and much physical risk have gone into contraception, yet few birth control counsellors consider the obvious option: give up on sexual intercourse and try the myriad alternatives for achieving sexual satisfaction for both partners.[18]

Sex is seen narrowly even when the point of the sex is pleasure, not reproduction. Is it a coincidence that sexuality is defined by and confined to sexual intercourse? In whose interests is it that sex be constructed in this way? Sexual intercourse may give women pleasure but there is no guarantee that it will. On the other hand, intercourse almost always gives sexual pleasure to men. The inequality of the arrangement is obvious. When Ann Landers asked her female readers whether they preferred cuddles to the act, no wonder no one questioned what the "act" referred to. What *is* remarkable is that her readers were still aware enough of their own bodies and their needs to protest that most of them, 72 per cent, said they would gladly exchange the act for some non-specific affection. They did not say they preferred to be cuddled because the Bible told them that fornication was a sin. They did not complain about the messiness of sex and semen and guck. Their problem was that they experienced sex as an act of power over them. They felt used and used up in sex. These women, in the face of an oppressive ideology locked firmly into our culture, are resisting. So were Ontario's legislators when they passed Bill 7, which included sexual orientation in the Human Rights Code. So is the feminist movement when it recognizes lesbians as an essential, perhaps central, force in a sexually conscious movement. So do men when they reject pornography and urge other men to do the same.

2

MANY PEOPLE, ENAMOURED OF the sentimental idea that we have freedom of choice in sexuality, reject these ideas and assume that everything is just fine as long as the participants mutually consent to these activities. Gayle Rubin, an outspoken critic of the feminist view that sexuality is socially constructed, is one of them. In "Talking Sex," the centrepiece for the pro-sex anthology *Pleasure and Danger*,[19] she describes violent sexual activities practiced by so-called "mutually consenting" partners as if there really is such a thing as consent. A female masochist who honestly describes pleasure in getting roughed up has not necessarily *chosen* the violence in a world that relentlessly promotes sexual subordination and patriarchal practices of abuse. If she emerges from sex bloodied and bruised, her orgasm has not cancelled her pain. She still needs the brutal force to feel pleasure. This is not consent, it is the internalized expression of sexual subordination.

Has the woman who escaped from child sexual abuse to the street and wound up turning tricks for a living consented to her life? Has the woman who learned sexuality as an incest victim consented to a sexuality in which she can get no pleasure unless she has no power? Has that fourteen-year-old who yearns so strongly to be accepted into an oppressive rock culture that she will be beaten up for the privilege really consented to the violence? Have those girls who know by age fifteen that looking good for boys is what life is all about consented to spending precious dollars on cosmetics and clothes? Have women who take what's given to them and make of it that sex is the only power game they can play consented to all of this? I think not.

Indeed, the perspective outlined here, the insistence on identifying and analyzing the prevailing sexual ideology that makes sexuality an experience of male power and female powerlessness, forces us to reconsider the notion of consent. Consent has real meaning only if we accept the liberal terms on sexuality. If we believe that there is a smorgasbord of sexual activities that people select at random, then consent does exist. But if we understand that social and sexual relations are constructed with the interests of male power at stake, if we accept that the socialization process begins at day one and never really lets up, if we understand that what distinguishes humans from any other animal is precisely our malleability and our ability to learn, then consent becomes a buzzword with very little sting. When ideology meets the body, consent no longer exists.

To understand the difference between a liberal view of sexuality and the feminist perspective presented here, think of a sexual spectrum of practices and sensibilities. Free-choice believers think the spectrum runs the gamut from heavy-duty sexual violence (apparently consensual) on one end to celibacy on the other. In the minds of those with a religious belief in consent, human beings are sprinkled equally along the spectrum.[20] But, like most liberals in general, most sex liberals *do* understand the dynamics of social institutions. They say that heterosexism and the imposed structure of marriage crowds the middle of the spectrum with heterosexual "loving" couples, leaving the minorities isolated at both ends. Advocates like Gayle Rubin insist that the people at the middle of the spectrum form a tyrannical majority with so little respect for the minority who celebrate sexual power, control and violence, that they would outlaw their practices. Rubin and her associates call for decriminalizing incest, calling it "intergenerational sex," and have developed a rhetoric that urges those people cluttering up the middle of the spectrum to liven up their sexual lives by trying some of these "outlawed" practices.

In contrast, I see the sexual spectrum running a gamut from the sexuality of dominance and submission on one end to a sexuality that eroticizes equality on the other. The prevailing sexual ideology operates in a way that locates most people on the side of dominance and submission. On the farthest end of the spectrum are women enslaved, bought, traded, imprisoned, abused and schooled in the art of submission so that they cannot tell the difference between their own pleasure and their own annihilation. Alongside them are the male sadists, the pimps, the abusers, the sexual obsessives who cannot tell the difference between their own sexual pleasure and the annihilation of another human being.

Moving away from the extreme end, towards the middle, yet still on the side of the prevailing ideology, are the women who can get on with their lives, who work, who love, who imagine themselves free, but who are still caught in the grips of the sexuality of subordination. Sometimes, in private, pornography turns them on. They frequently cannot stand the men they are attracted to. Often they have the best sex after they argue with their lovers. They like to tease because sexual tension turns everybody on. They do things for their partners because they suspect that if sex is the only way men can know intimacy, then they will have to take all the "intimacy" they can get. Near them on the spectrum are men who live their lives, who work, who love, who imagine themselves free. They subscribe to *Penthouse* because they like to look at the perfect bodies of women who have been made available to them. They ask their lovers to wear the kind of lingerie that makes women look like the objects in pornography, because knowing women will reduce themselves that way increases men's sense of power. When these men get angry, they want to have sex. When they have sex, they close their eyes and concentrate on the pleasure they get from slicing through a woman; they forget they have a partner. Sometimes all of this goes on in their heads without their lovers knowing it. But it still goes on and on. Because we do not know what it would be like living outside the sway of patriarchal sexual ideology, we don't know where individuals would fall on this spectrum of sexuality if there *were* such a thing as sexual choice. As long as we have not been released from the grip of the sexuality of dominance and submission, most of us are located somewhere between the middle of the spectrum and the end where sexual slavery is enshrined.

This view of sexuality leads to a fresh perspective on the place of sadomasochism in our culture, and it has caused deep divisions within some circles of the gay and women's liberation movements. Many gay and lesbian activists have criticized any analyses that tend to question sadomasochistic sexuality. They bemoan the absence of sexual pluralism in society and the vulnerability of sexual minorities who have been denied their personal freedom. Those espousing sex liberalism say these dissidents are the real revolutionaries challenging sexual norms.[21] But contrary to their personal claims about their sexuality, the practitioners of sadomasochism who inflict and experience humiliation and pain in closely scripted encounters are not at all sexual dissidents, but proponents of the dominant sexual ideology.

So-called "tops" and "bottoms" in the lesbian sadomasochistic sexual construct fiddle with roles but they do not challenge the construct. Theirs is same-sex activity and they often trade roles, thus operating outside of male/female expectations, and proving that the dominant/submissive pattern is not biologically based. But except for their lesbianism, they are not in a minority. They are close to the extreme end of the continuum of the sexual majority. They may call themselves liberators, radical perverts, sexual outlaws or anything else, but they are really some of the most eloquent proponents of the sexual status quo.

Sex-critical feminists believe that these practices do not just fall from heaven but are constructed by social expectations and personal experience. In response, Gayle Rubin hotly contests the dominance of the sexuality of subordination. "Variation is a fundamental property of life," she insists, and sexuality is no different.[22] Rubin's near-religious conviction that variation is a fundamental property of sex is the last word in sex liberalism, producing bald statements whose basis has never been researched, let alone proven. The content of pornography, on the other hand, has been closely analyzed, giving us insights into sexual patterns and their influence both on consumers and on other forms of culture. Sex liberals could sit for days on end combing the products of culture for erotic materials that fall outside the erotic system described above, but they would not be able to find the "alternative" as many times as they uncover the prevailing sexual values. They certainly would not see a wide spectrum of sexual presentation, because that sexual variation simply does not exist in actual practice.

A key source of resistance to the idea that sexuality is political or gendered are the sociobiologically-influenced ideologues who are convinced that whatever shape or structure exists in sexuality is constructed by nature and biology. Because we experience sex in our bodies, it is tempting to believe that whatever our bodies do is natural. But therein lies the overwhelming power of sexual ideology: it does not work on the level of ideas, it works right in our bodies, making it seem not like a constructed set of social values, but like another natural fact of life. Sex organs are part of the biological package and they are designed to function in a particular way for a particular purpose, namely reproduction. Thus the biology factor can feed into sex liberal perspectives as well, allowing for the assumption that sexual pleasure, no matter how it feels and no matter what patterns it may fall into, exists as a reproductive given, proto-social, untrammelled by patriarchal systems of male dominance and unrelated to the way society is organized.

However, regardless of what it takes to reproduce, thousands of women are getting pregnant with barely a quiver from their genital regions. So, the biological demands of reproduction are not defining sexual pleasure. Something else is. New discoveries in science indicate biology does not determine as much as sociobiologists tell us. Endocrinologists are discovering that hormones, the byproducts of biological sex, are essential factors in the crossover from biology to the behaviours that create society. Biology is not at all the discrete phenomenon many people think it is.

And really, if male dominance and female submission are so natural, why does there have to be constant pressure to conform? Why the ubiquitous promotion for male power and female powerlessness in sex? Is our biology so fragile that it cannot be left to act "naturally" on its own? Perhaps ideology does not create sexuality but reflect what nature gives us. But how do we know what nature gives us when the "pinkification" of girls and the "blueing" of boys start on day one? The truth is that we don't know, and we will never find out until we free ourselves from the chains of the dominant sexual ideology.

When ideology grinds away at our physical being, we lose sense of our bodily integrity, and bodily integrity is fundamental to humanness. As long as it is violated, warped, constructed by political forces, we are less than human, stumbling down a sexual road somebody else built for us. No, say sex liberals. They warn that the deep analysis of sex developed by sex-critical feminism will scare women away from sex and throw them back into a Victorian or 50s-style sexual regime in which sexuality is an underground activity.[23] For these pro-sex ideologues, the operative sexual ideology of patriarchy is repression, not oppression. Many of the most influential proponents of sex liberalism were reared in the 50s, and are angry at how the values of that decade thwarted sexuality and frustrated an entire generation of women. But these writers are using Victorian and 50s models as if they were the norm, when in fact they are culturally specific experiences, even in western terms. The French never went through a Victorian period, and the term "the 50s" resonates with sexual propriety only in North America. Both periods are actually historical anomalies that are not at all representative of the way sexuality has been practiced over the past 100 years.

The sexual revolution of the 60s and 70s eclipsed the 50s' repression, but it failed miserably to produce the liberation it promised. In fact, the conditions during those periods tended to support the values structure and practices of sexual subordination. As the clarion call went out for free love, women were suddenly expected to have sex lest they be tagged with the label "unliberated" and become social pariahs. For many of us, the sexual revolution was really a smoke screen for what felt like forced sex and an experience of having sex shoved down our throats.

In the 80s we have come into a new phase. Women are encouraged to have sex for themselves, to reclaim their sexuality, to take care of it, to think of sex as something that can transform our lives. Conferences abound on female sexuality. Headlines blare the news that women have discovered sex. Now, instead of female abstinence or female disinterest or females putting up with it, women are apparently enjoying sex like never before. Pornographers report that women's interest in their products is increasing, but at the same time women are not demanding that the pornography change to accommodate different values and feelings. In fact, women are becoming better socialized into the paradigm of male dominance and female submission. Lesbian pornography in magazines like On Our Backs has become a growth industry, subordinating women for the pleasure of a lesbian readership. There is no doubt that female orgasm is alive and well, but women's rediscovery of sex has taken place within the limited frame of the patriarchal sexual ideology.

You can see the painful limitations of "the new sexuality" in the new female erotica on the market. Lonnie Barbach, a psychologist and sex counsellor, decided to celebrate women's rediscovery of sex by publishing women's erotic experiences and fantasies in her book Pleasures: Women Write Erotica.[24] Anyone who imagines that male dominance and female submission are the stuff of male literature only will be astonished by Barbach's text. The book provides ample evidence that the prevailing erotic system has closed to perfection: where before only men got turned on to sexual subordination and male power, now women too can get tuned into female submission and male power. Consider:

"The sensation of being completely at his mercy, of my legs begging to grip him, until the pulsing stabs sent me into my own world of ecstacy," (from "The Way He Captured Me").

"Fausto was the only man to understand just how much this spot made me vulnerable, a slave to his passionate touch," (from "How I Spent my Summer Vacation").

"One of his glances would tell me to follow him, to speak or to join him in play. All his commands and wishes I obeyed with a willingness that came from inside. My obedience was not willed, it was instinctual."

"Andre spoke in a voice insistent and sure. There was a dark tone of threat in it, which made my skin tingle. 'Come now,' he commanded. And my orgasm came like gusts of tropical rain." (Both from "After I Submit.")

These women are in the throes of sexual subordination. They are stabbed by penises and are at the mercy of their male partners, happy to submit to their enslavement. They come on command, assume it is natural and beg for more. These are typical of the stories in Barbach's anthology (Susan Griffen's wonderful story of a lost relationship is hopelessly out of place). *Pleasures* is not fiction, but the lived sexuality of these women writers. Is this really progress? Is an orgasm worth all of this self-annihilation? This so-called erotica sounds more like sexual abuse than anything else. This is an especially nauseating proposition given that sexual abuse is a virtual epidemic, something women fear and despise. The paeans to sexual subordination in Barbach's book are an insult to women whose sexuality has been misshapen by rape. Or perhaps hidden in *Pleasures* is a new strategy for surviving sexual abuse: eroticize it.

In the meantime, sex liberals blithely declare that "what works (sexually) is what's good." What they mean is that what works is what feels good and that as long as women get pleasure in sex, social change cannot be far behind. But what feels good is constructed by sexual oppression, by a system that makes sexual abuse inevitable, and an ideology that is certain to keep women down. Given the way pro-sex ideologues have turned their backs on any systemic analysis, the term pro-sex is being as badly abused by these sex-at-all-costs advocates as the term pro-life has been misappropriated by the anti-abortion movement. And so, in the same way that feminists conceded the term pro-life to the anti-choice movement, knowing advocates for choice were the ones who really cared about the quality of life, those striving to create real sexual liberation will have to concede the term pro-sex to those whose vision cannot see beyond patriarchal limits. Let's call ourselves sex-critical and agree that when it comes to sex, we'd rather be, well, pro-choice.

3

FEMINISM IS NOT a struggle against sexuality, it is the struggle for change in the sexual arena. This frightens many people. Because they imagine that they have their own sexuality, as if it were a personal possession imprinted with their unique personality, they interpret a call for sexual transformation as a statement that there is something wrong with them. They feel personally attacked. They listen to a critique of pornography and start looking over their shoulders for the sex police. So when Murial Dimen, in "Politically Correct, Politically Incorrect" (*Pleasure and Danger*), says that "sexual intimacy is resistant to rules of political correctness" and when Gayle Rubin agrees that sexuality cannot be expected to operate on a single standard, they turn the point around. They worry that sex-critical feminists have a sexual agenda that they will be forced to follow, when the rules for what sex is and how sexual intimacy will be acted have already been forced on them by the dominant sexual ideology. They should understand that responding sexually to pornography, or getting turned on by any other elements that promote the sexuality of subordination, does not mark anyone as sick, depraved or morally corrupt. It does not have to mark them as an enemy. But it does mark them as perfectly socialized into the patriarchal erotic system.

A sexual agenda for liberation is the sexual agenda of resistance to this erotic system. In the same way as feminism in its early stages urged every person to examine the ways in which she or he had become part of the sexist status quo, feminism now has to ask how we can dismantle and rebuild our sexual lives in a way that will free us of the chains of male dominance and female submission. Andrea Dworkin has referred to this as the search for real sexual intelligence.[25] Envisioning such a movement, creating it, yearning for it, has nothing to do with establishing sex stormtroopers bent on scrutinizing every bedroom in the country. There are no censors here, only people passionately committed to deepening the explorations of how patriarchal systems of sexuality have stolen our physical beings.

We have a long way to go before we uncover the full extent of the damage. We may not see the full repair in our lifetimes and it may not be possible to chart the entire course for change. In my own travels I am constantly asked to reel off the full agenda. I cannot do that. But rather than leave readers with a sense that the task is too daunting, let me sketch out a few thoughts on strategies that might get the process going.

The first step in creating change is to identify the ways in which sexuality is gendered and politicized. This book is part of that process. Another part of the process involves the painful work of actually reading or looking at pornography. It's amazing how many people make up their minds about pornography without confronting the subject matter. This has done a great deal to distort the issues, for these people tend to develop their opinions on pornography based on their fear of excessive solutions to the problem rather than on a clear understanding of what the problem actually is.

Let me give one intriguing example. A criminologist at Laurentian University completed a study on Canadian standards of tolerance by surveying a group of Ontarians. She reported that not only were these standards much more liberal than the legal standard for obscenity, which proscribed the distribution of depictions of almost all explicit sexuality, but that women shared only slightly less liberal standards than the men surveyed. This criminologist planned to testify as an expert witness in obscenity cases in support of the accused. She also hoped that her study would influence new legislation and ease anti-pornography laws.

The researcher had distributed a questionnaire to her subject group asking them whether they had problems with the depictions of various sexual acts. When I asked her if she had shown her subject group pornography containing any of these practices, she said no. So it was all really a useless abstract exercise. It turned out that her study tapped the fears people have of saying anything bad about sex itself, of appearing illiberal about sex, and not their feelings about pornography.[26]

Researcher James Check studies the effects of pornography on male subjects. A crucial part of his method — and one that responds to some of the ethical concerns about showing pornography to random males — is the debriefing process in which he discusses his findings with his subjects. Through the debriefing process, he describes what the experiments were about and the meaning of the results. He reports that his debriefing is an eye-opener, and that it has been extremely useful in raising his subjects' awareness of what pornography has done to their attitudes and feelings.

For my part, I tend not to show or read pornography during public educationals. Partly this is because in these circumstances, critics invariably accuse anti-pornography activists of selecting only the most grisly pornographic samples. These people usually do not want to face the truth about what pornography actually looks like. Also, some men come to pornography lectures only to see the pornography and I am not interested in participating in their voyeurism. But the main reason I do not show pornography is because it upsets audiences so much that they cannot listen or think or reason. Upon seeing the materials, most people can only think of extreme censorship solutions and of widening police powers.

But there are ways of reviewing pornography in situations that are safe and which generate rather than prevent discussion.

Groups can be formed to work on the project. Although gender-mixed groups could work on decoding pornography, they would have to consist of people who are comfortable with each other and who can talk openly. Usually, all-women or all-male groups create the best conditions for this kind of work. Throughout the process, there has to be room for participants to express their anger, but they also must have room to discuss the ways in which the pornography works for them sexually. It is infuriating to see how pornography uses women, but it is equally enraging to come to the realization that pornography co-opts all of us. We have to be able to say these things in an atmosphere that is not judgemental, or the work of deconstruction cannot take place properly.

The process of decoding has to begin at as early an age as possible. This strategy is already being developed through media literacy courses from kindergarten through high school. Through media literacy, students learn the economics of media, what constitutes a market, the construction of images and the ideological messages that underlie them. Although media literacy can cover everything from newspapers to soap operas, the Association for Media Literacy in Ontario urges that a unit on sexuality in the media be included in all media curricula. The *Resource Book on Media Literacy*, written by a team of media teachers in conjunction with Ontario Federation of Teachers and the Ministry of Education, contains a comprehensive unit on sexuality. It facilitates the kind of classroom discussion that gets young people at all levels involved in discussing sex and sexual roles. I have undertaken some of this teaching myself,[27] and the results have been astonishing. The materials — rock videos, ads, feature films, any media that the students know inside out — combined with an interactive teaching method create a dynamic discussion in which peers get to talk in ways they have never done before.

I led a media training session with grade twelve students where an energetic discussion took place about an advertment for Impulse perfume. It beings with a woman taking an escalator in Toronto's Eaton Centre. As she ascends, a man taking the descending escalator passes her and is enchanted, presumably by her perfume. He races to the flower store, buys a bouquet and then proceeds to tear through the mall, chasing after the woman.

When he finally catches up with her, she accepts the bouquet and smiles with appreciation.

To help make the distinction between fantasy and reality, I suggested that the girls put themselves in the woman's position. "What would you do if a man you did not know started chasing you through the Eaton's Centre?" I asked.

"I'd be terrified and I'd split, as fast as possible," said one young woman, rolling her eyes.

"Wait a second," said one of the boys incredulously. "Don't tell me if a good-looking guy started pursuing you in a mall, you wouldn't like it." He grinned. "If a good-looking girl started coming after me I'd be thrilled."

"Well, it's different for us," said another girl. "It's just not the same." So flew the sparks in a class on media and sexuality. Through the course of the discussion, the students talked about how the advertisement was constructed almost entirely from a male point of view. They began to see how media products thrive on fantasy. But most important, they engaged in a no-holds-barred discussion about sexual violence. For what may have been the first time, young men listened to young women talk about their fears, and the girls listened while the boys slowly began to grasp that they simply did not have the same experience as their female counterparts. With a few subtle hints from me, they were able to see that a nude stranger presenting himself to a woman is seen as a threat, while a nude stranger presenting herself to a man is seen as an opportunity.

In another class of grade twelve students, I showed a number of heavy metal rock videos in which the exploitation and dehumanization of women were fairly obvious. In this instance, before we could begin the decoding, students made it clear that they were wholly disdainful of the heavy metal genre. In a way this was a good thing, since it meant we could proceed without offending anyone's personal tastes. I asked the students to make a list of all the things the women were doing in the video (usually not much, except for standing there as objects), the number of violent acts (many), the gender of the perpetrators (almost always male) and the gender of the victims (usually female). The students got the message.

Then I showed a soft-focus video featuring a handsome male singer anticipating his upcoming date with a very beautiful woman. At first the students were confused. There was no overt violence, no women in cages, no head-banging. The content was not that disturbing. But basing my method on feminist theories of representation, I was able to show that there were issues of form rather than just content to be considered. The video presented a narrative entirely from the point of view of the male singer. As the narrative progressed we watched the female object of desire in her bathroom preparing for the evening. Throughout the video she appeared significantly less clad than he did. The students were able to discuss how the video transformed romance into an exercise in inequality, turning the viewer into an intrusive voyeur. For the students, all of this was a revelation. They were learning to look past the surface of the story-line to the way images are constructed.

The last video in the unit featured Bruce Springsteen in a live performance of one of his most popular songs. The frame contained only Springsteen, dressed in a white T-shirt and jeans, singing "Fire." The class was now completely miffed. Where was the violence? Where were the more subtle forms of objectification? In the lyrics, I said, bringing the discussion back to a different element of content. "I'm driving in my car/ You turn on the radio/ I'm holding you close/ You just say no/ You say you don't like it/ I know you're a liar/ 'Cause when we kiss ... fire." Immediately, the students knew what was going on. "He's raping her," said one, so quickly that I was shocked. "No means no," said another. It turned out that the class had discussed forced sex in a sex education class, and other media studies had familiarized them with rape myths. Sex education and media literacy together were creating the kind of awareness that could eliminate the future market for pornography.

Since sex made its way onto the feminist agenda in the early 80s, feminists have been looking for a way to define sexuality in their own terms. Making sexuality visible in images and in culture — a cultural offensive, as some activists have called it[28] — has been turned into a high priority for feminist artists and anti-censorship advocates. Although it is certainly naive to imagine that the small magazines and the eight-millimeter films feminists create could ever compete with a pornography industry with more outlets than McDonald's, I do think that creating alternative erotica has the potential to be an empowering strategy. The problem is, how?

Alternative erotica is hard to find and extremely hard to make. Much of the so-called feminist materials spewed out over the past five years reproduces the conventions and subordinating practices of pornography.[29] This is because putting a woman behind the camera or at the typewriter describing sexuality does not make the product an alternative, any more than urging women to have sex within the ideological frame of subordination can change sexuality itself.

A Toronto exhibit of erotic pottery by five women contained more than 200 pieces. All but a handful of the pieces represented female sexual parts. Even though the artists were all heterosexual, they reproduced the centuries-old convention that women and women only equal sex, and that the penis was too sacred or profane to present.

A new calendar is now available that features women in sexually explicit poses. The calendar is for lesbians. But with the exception of some of the text beneath the pictures, there is no difference between this new item geared to gay women and *Playboy*'s calendar, or the *Sports Illustrated* swimsuit calendar, although the lesbian product is a bit more sexually explicit. Look at the new lesbian pornography like *On Our Backs*. It features lesbians in sadomasochistic scenarios and appropriates the man-made language that describes sexual oppression. The editors imagine that just by saying the same words, women can change them. They are dreaming.

Besides, just as pornography is a practice beyond the images it produces, so is creating erotica. This means that we have to ask the same questions about erotica as we asked about pornography. Who are the women (and men) in the materials? How did they get there? What is our relationship to them? An experiment sponsored by the A Space gallery in Toronto made these questions extremely compelling. The gallery funded a number of activists and artists in a project designed to create an alternative erotic film language. One thoughtful feminist who took these issues seriously was almost completely sabotaged by her inability to find any women to appear in her film. By the time she had gone through her phone book, tapped the resources of all the performers she knew, and promised that they would not be compromised, only to be refused again and again, she realized that the only women she could get to appear were women already in the sex trade. She understood that to use them was to use them. Determined not to reproduce the oppressive inequalities of pornography, she wound up choosing the only really ethical option: she appeared in the film herself, and in the end, the only sexually explicit thing about the film was the spoken text. Another artist involved in the project solved the problem the same way, by going on camera herself with her male partner.

The fact is that most women feel that having sex on camera would be a violating and invasive experience. No amount of sex-positive rhetoric or well-meaning talk about the "cultural offensive" changes their minds. One woman who did appear in one of the films said later that she felt that people never really looked at her in the same way again. Barbara Hammer, who broke some of the ground in the area of female-centred erotica, came to a conference in Peterborough, Ontario, in 1981 to show sexually explicit films in which she herself appeared, and wept before they were shown. She suddenly felt terribly vulnerable. These experiences are real and have to be taken seriously in the flush of exuberance that has accompanied the drive to create alternative erotica.

I ask specific questions of male users of *Playboy* and *Penthouse* who think their practice is harmless. Would you take off your clothes and pose for a camera? Who do you think does? Why should you have access to the sexuality of women less fortunate than you? Any time a person gets turned on by somebody doing something he would never do himself, there is subordination taking place. The same is true of the new women- and lesbian-made erotica. Do we know how much *On Our Backs* and the other lesbian eroticists pay women to be in the materials? The sad truth is that if we apply the same standards to these new materials as we apply to pornography, we discover that the new erotica is merely a variation on pornography's theme. Many women have said that sexually explicit materials have played an important role in their sexual growth. Lesbians in particular have been desperate for a visual or textual validation of their sexuality, and have eagerly snapped up any materials they can get their hands on. Are we interested in multiplying the amount of sexual exploitation that exists? Are we interested in creating new markets, or is one step forward for the consumer — sexual growth — become two steps back for the women subordinated in the materials that turn us on? I think that in the larger scheme of things we really get no place if we grow sexually off the backs of other women.

If we release our bodies and minds from the grip of the prevailing sexual ideology, whether it is in pornography, our own alternative erotica or anywhere else in our lives, we will find out what sexuality without all the patriarchal baggage looks like and feels like. We will find out that sexual possibilities are much wider than we experience them now and that we don't actually belong on that far end of sexuality's spectrum, where dominance and submission prevail. But releasing the grip is only the first step in the process of sexual liberation. Finding an *alternative* to the sexuality of subordination is central to the movement for sexual liberation, an alternative that moves us to the other end of the spectrum: I yearn to live in a world that eroticizes equality instead of hierarchy, violence, dominance and submission.

All of these explorations — the critique of pornography, the critique of alternative erotica, the critique of sexuality and especially the call to eroticize equality — have generated astonishing assumptions: many people confuse sex-critical thinking with anti-sex attitudes and a call for celibacy. After a speech on sexuality in which I suggested that we eroticize equality, one writer in a pro-sex newspaper reported that I had advocated celibacy. At another panel on sexuality in which I had spent considerable time on the same subject, a questioner, convinced that sex could be only one way, asked me why I didn't talk about sex.

These comments speak volumes on the way existing sexual ideology has trapped our sexual imaginations. If the analysis were of something else, like, say, food production, the response would probably not be the same. If I explained how we have lost control over what food goes into our mouths; if I analyzed the way junk food and white sugar are promoted as if they had protein value; if I explained how middle-agents inflate the cost of food so that certain economic interests could increase their capital gains; if I described how our bodies have adjusted to chemicals and preservatives that are really highly toxic; if I demonstrated how these and other poisons have been made to taste good, no one would say that I was telling people to stop eating. Yet, when it comes to sex, people have a hard time thinking of any alternative to the existing patriarchal erotic system other than celibacy.

Actually, celibacy is a perfectly valid strategy for dealing with sexual oppression. For many women, and an increasing number of men, temporarily saying "no" to sexual activity, creating a clean slate on which to draw sexual desire, is an important part of the process. Sheila Jeffreys has documented the historical relationship between spinstership and the movement for women's rights, suggesting that in the first wave of feminism, one could not exist without the other.[30] Today the issues have changed somewhat. For some survivors of abuse, sex is simply too hard. For some refugees from the 60s who feel like the sexuality has been pumped out of them, abstaining for a period is just what they need to sort out their sexual priorities. These people are growing more and more alienated as feminists make their erotica and urge women to get as much sex as possible. For people trying to transform sexuality through abstinence, the new pro-sex feminism feels like another version of forced sex. I think celibacy — staying away from subordinating sex, especially to make room for imaginings on an equality-oriented alternative — can be a first step in sexual liberation, but only for some. And although I do not believe it is a complete strategy, I think it is important to respect those who choose it.

While celibate women and men are called uptight prudes, many lesbian women have developed a kind of chauvinism that leads them to believe that their sexual choice in itself subverts the sexuality of subordination. This is a delusion that has to be dispelled. It may be true that lesbianism can form the basis for an alternative to patriarchal sexuality, but that does not mean that the sexuality of male dominance and female submission cannot operate effectively within the same-sex model. Lesbians practicing sadomasochism will attest to that, and the proliferation of lesbian pornography supports Andrea Dworkin's contention that lesbians break only one of the myriad rules that keep us hooked into the sexuality of subordination.[31] The kind of self-examination required to create the sexuality of liberation is as important to lesbians as it is to heterosexual men and women.

Some women have suggested that the real alternative is to create a sexuality that subordinates men. They say that they feel empowered when they turn men into objects and when they exercise sexual power over their male partners. Indeed, many lesbians in sadomasochistic relationships have said outright that being a "top" (the current term for the dominant partner), and even being a "bottom" in a scripted encounter controlled by the participants, is a necessary antidote to the powerlessness they feel in the world. But turning men into objects does not change the system, it merely gives women a new way to prop up the ideology of dominance and submission. And the lesbians who trade places in their sadomasochistic sexual games change sex as much as making a woman chief executive officer of General Motors changes capitalism. To stretch a metaphor, we need more than just a an equal share of the patriarchal pie, we have to change the pie's flavour, its ingredients, its texture, its shape. It is certainly tempting to imagine another millennium in which men are as oppressed by women as women have been by men. But ultimately, turning the tables in sex is to eroticizing equality what revenge is to justice.

So what *is* the sexuality of liberation? What is the true alternative? This is a question that only a movement of sexual activists can research. Along with others, I have begun my own investigation, and although it barely scratches the surface of our sexual potential, it may inspire others to embark on a similar exploration.

To start with, we need a new language. Sheila Jeffreys has suggested that we stop referring to orgasm as pleasure, since pleasure does not adequately describe women's complex reactions and ambivalent feelings towards the experience.[32] In other contexts, completely new words would be wonderful but even the exercise of exchanging subordinating concepts for liberating ones might be useful. Why, for example, are we so obssessed with sexual power? "There is power in all sexual relationships," many feminists have been heard to intone. Why not consider the word "energy" instead? "I can't get turned on unless I feel vulnerable," say others. But the language is in their way. If they exchanged the word "vulnerable" for "open," they might feel better about the source of their desire.

Intent in sex has to be closely examined. It does not necessarily have to be shared but it helps if it is mutually acknowledged. Men (and women) can track their patterns of dominance with some basic questions. Are you doing something to an object when you are feeling sexual or are you doing something with a partner? Are you doing something for your own ego, to work out your own fears and anger with no thoughts for the person with you, or are you being sexual to communicate? Are you having sex to use someone or to explore with someone? Do your feelings go beyond your penis?

Women (and men) who are striving to emerge out of a pattern of submissiveness might begin to question closely the source of their desire. Do you feel spent after sex or energized? Do you confuse your partners' anger with love? Is love something you fall into or do you carry yourself into it? When your legs are spread, do you feel incomplete, like a hole to be stopped up, or ready to meet someone? Do you cry or laugh? Do you really want to be there?

The patriarchal terms for sexuality have to be reversed, inverted or transformed. For me, it means that the thrill of danger, violence and threats in sex will give way to the conditions of safety where real freedom of expression can exist. It means that the sexual tension created by undercurrents and unspoken desires will give way to a outright honesty that nurtures communication and trust. It means that the titillation of bathroom sex and fast fucks with strangers will give way to a love between people who are not afraid to let someone else see inside their hearts.

How would the world look, how would it feel if as much time, money and creativity as are spent on eroticizing power, hierarchy, violence, male dominance and female submission were spent on a truly transformative project like eroticizing equality? The world of eroticized equality is so far away from so much of our experience that we can barely imagine it, let alone start creating it. Sometimes it seems hopelessly beyond our grasp. But despair is the easy way out. Somewhere beyond the pro-sex disdain of Pat Califia, who says eroticizing equality doesn't pass her "wet test,"[33] and the hopelessness of militant feminists who say we should not bother trying, there has to be a way to create this world. The sexual crisis we face has been driven by a political forces that are dehumanizing, yes, but also human. The perfect sexual system of male dominance and female submission is a human achievement of politics. It can be broken by a sexual and political movement of human spirits.

In the world of eroticized equality these spirits do not know sexual destruction.

They touch each other and live.

APPENDIX

Book Review, *Canadian Journal of Women and the Law*, Vol. 1, No. 1, 1985.

Women Against Censorship. Edited by Varda Burstyn. Vancouver: Douglas and McIntyre, 1985.

By now I must have heard hundreds of Canadians try to talk about pornography. Mostly they do not talk. They fulminate, they cry, they panic. They do so, I think, because pornography brings together so many matters that cut to the very root of our everyday experience and to the very heart of feminism's central political and theoretical issues: sexuality and power. Feminists have discovered that experience and theory are not separate things. I wish I could say the same for *Women Against Censorship.*

The main concerns of this recently released Canadian publication are the impact of mass media, alternative erotica, the relationship between feminism and the state, the relationship between women and the state, and the miseries of state censorship. You will probably notice that missing from this catalogue is the issue that galvanized the publication of *Women Against Censorship* in the first place — pornography. In *Women Against Censorship*, pornography is either avoided, misconstrued or trivialized to the point that it becomes invisible in the text. This is not willful manipulation. Some of it stems from the writers' passionate views on censorship. Having decided that censorship is a terrible thing, it became necessary for the contributors to argue backwards from that fear to the conclusion that pornography is not so dreadful. Sometimes even when a writer eloquently describes the problem of pornography, as does June Callwood,[1] it gets lost in a defense of civil liberties. As should be fairly plain, *Women Against Censorship* do not speak with a unanimous voice.[2] Quite the contrary. Often one writer's arguments are refuted in the very next article by another writer who takes the opposite position.[3] This turns out to be an effective editorial strategy. It gives the impression of multiple viewpoints that converge at the one point on which all the writers can agree: censorship is bad.

Ironically, had *Women Against Censorship* given us more of real women's experience, I think they would have given a more complete argument against state control. Consider this: in the spring of 1984, feminist artists in Toronto were invited to make films that would develop an alternative erotic film language. The films were not sexually explicit, though some of them depicted sexual activity like kissing and fondling. One of the most compelling anti-censorship arguments I have ever heard came from one of these filmmakers. She had included in her film a scene showing her kissing her lesbian lover. The artists never intended to submit the films to the Ontario censor board (all screenings were held in private), but what if the police had battered down the door and seized the film anyway? The thought of then-attorney general Roy McMurtry and members of the vice squad watching this movie was a nauseating one. I knew these women and I understood this artist's trauma. *Women Against Censorship* should have described this kind of experience.

Lisa Steele is a video artist who has already experienced harassment at the hands of the police who are trying to interfere with the distribution of her videos. I would have found an account of what that harassment feels like much more useful than the article she did write, which belittles the impact of pornography in the world.[4] What I am trying to say is that there *are* important things to be said about the exercise of state authority. *Women Against Censorship* do not say those things, largely, I would venture, because it is crucial to these writers to keep the discussion abstract. They do not want to get too close to what really happens to artists who have actually experienced censorship because they would have to notice what really happens to women in pornography.

Pornography, as I have come to know it, is the practice of

presenting, trafficking and consuming sexual subordination for sexual pleasure. Sexual subordination is promoted through an $8 billion industry on this continent; this industry requires real traffic in real women in order to produce pornography. What pornographers do is keep women[5] sexually subordinated so that they can record sex — sometimes it looks more like atrocities — which consumers (mostly men) in this practice can use to get sexually turned on. This is what pornography is and does. Pornography is not, as *Women Against Censorship* insist, images. Referring to pornography as images or as pictures is a convenient way of distancing us all from what pornography means to the real women who are in the pornography and to the real women who have to deal with pornography's consumers. Sara Diamond's essay is the only article that really attempts to analyze pornography. The essay is laced with euphemisms: "images" instead of documents; sexual "representation" instead of presentation; men shown "symbolically" controlling women, rather than actually subordinating them; a hefty dose of Freudian analysis and film theory as well as the declarative statement that it is a mistake to say that "images of sex are the same as real sex."

Why these distinctions? To the women who are in the pictures, it *is* real sex; it happened to them; it is their lives.[6] To the women who are forced by consumers to look at the pornography, or forced to imitate the sex in the pictures, it *becomes* sex in their real lives.[7] More crucially, to the men who get erections while looking at the materials, this *is* sex for them. Academic discussions of the camera's tendency to distort time and perspective cannot change or obscure the experience of real women and men in the practice of pornography.

I agree that images are not the real problem. Pornographers are. Focussing on the images and neglecting the process of production and consumption of pornography keeps the discussion tied to the pictures. The discussion thus ignores the first half of reality. Pornographers make the pictures. Regardless of anything else, and especially regardless of anyone's generous interpretation of what the pictures mean, pornographers are trying to do something in particular. *Women Against Censorship* seem to want to avoid this fact. I sense their avoidance when I read the discussion of the "one-third" principle.[8] Carole Vance and her co-authors contend that one-third of all people are sexually aroused by sexually explicit materials, one-third are repulsed and one-third have no reaction whatsoever. Relying on these unsupported statistics, they conclude that censorship would be undemocratic. But this kind of analysis ignores the fact that pornographers will do almost anything to women in order to give one-third of the male population the sexual pleasure they are buying. Besides, if sexual pluralism reigns supreme, why do so many of the products of pornography look the same? What do we do with a population of entrepreneurs who are trying to turn men on to sexual subordination? What do we do with the fact that they are having such spectacular success?

While attempting to understand the process of consumption in the practice of pornography, Sara Diamond rejects outright the so-called behaviourist approach. "The suggestion," she says, "that consumers of pornographic material or other media products respond in zombie-like imitative fashion to all powerful images [sic] is both false and frightening."[9] I agree that it is frightening. But how can she say it is false when she knows (or ought to know) that advertisers spend $1 billion a year on the assumption that many people in their audiences will be moved by *images* to drive or walk to the nearest store and buy the advertised product? How can she say that it is false, when women have been talking to shelter workers about how they are terrorized by men who force sex on them when those men bring pornography into the home? How can it be false, when sadomasochistic magazines are crammed with advertisements for paraphernalia — whips, leather and the rest of the weapons that men need in order to get the sex that is advertised in the magazines? Often, as in the case of *Hustler* magazine, the now defunct *Canadian Elite* magazine, and (possibly) the lesbian magazine *On Our Backs*, the publishers have an economic interest in the sex toy companies that provide the mail order service. In other words, the pornographers have a specific *stake* in making sure that the consumer acts out the sex shown in the pornography.

Even if we assume that real women do not have to act out sexually subordinating sex for or with consumers of pornography, we cannot continue to deny that pornographers force real women to participate in making the images in the first place. These real women are almost as invisible in *Women Against Censorship* as they are in pornography itself. Even if the real women who live with pornography consumers are "safe," the constant consumption of pornography ensures that it will continue to be profitable to produce pornography. And whenever pornography is produced, real women experience sexual coercion, economic coercion and sexual subordination.

One strategy for neutralizing feminist critiques of pornography is to indicate that every other kind of mass media is at least as dangerous. Both Lisa Steele and Myrna Kostash employ this tactic.[10] Both articles are very useful, and better still, they are feminist to the core, for they analyze mass media and explain how pernicious the products of popular culture can be. This is *Women Against Censorship's* contribution to the "slippery slope" argument. "Where," Kostash seems to be asking, "can we reasonably draw the line?"[11] We could draw the line at the specific eroticization of sexual inequality. June Callwood is afraid that legislation that catches "pornography that shows the mutilation of women could also be applied to war coverage of the news."[12] This fear is poorly founded. Newscasters report the news. They are not committed first and foremost to giving men erections. Or we could draw the line at the point where pornographers brag, as they do in advertising snuff[13] films, that they trade in the torture of women. Certainly pornographers know the difference between working on 42nd Street in New York and working on Madison Avenue, or they would be advertizers working on Madison Avenue. Still, the products of western industrialized culture are permeated with the evidence of sexual inequality on which sexism and capitalism depend. As one anti-pornography activist and feminist theorist put it, "the liberal's slippery slope is the feminist totality."[14]

Lisa Steele makes the cultural argument in a different way. "If you think pornography is the central problem facing women today, I urge you to watch TV for about two days."[15] Few feminists do in fact refer to pornography as women's "central" problem. However, Lisa Steele's attack on almost all of the products of

cultural industries is a wonderful indictment of the sex stereotyping in popular culture. But she looks only at the pictures. She
does not see the conditions under which cultural products are
manufactured. She does not seem to be aware that the types of
sexual subordinations that real women in these industries experience *matters* to these women. I am almost certain that the
casting couch *is* a fixture everywhere in the entertainment
business. But in pornography there is often rape, assault and drug
addiction on the casting couch. Admittedly, the difference between the sexual harassment in "sleep-with-me-or-you-won't-get-
the-TV-spot" that pervades advertising agencies, and the rape in
"smile-you-bitch-or-I'll-kill-you" that goes on on pornography is a
matter of degree, but I think the degree matters.

Most mass media present sexual stereotypes as entertaining,
but they do not present the actual sexual harassment that may
have gone into the making of a mass media product as the entertainment itself. Pornography does a great deal of sex stereotyping
of its own, but it does more than that. It turns men on to putting
women down. Is there really *no* difference between a snuff film
and a ring-around-the-collar advertisement for Wisk detergent?
Certainly both are advertisements: one advertises a cleaning product and the other advertises sexual subordination. Both, in the
long run, are advertisements for sexual inequality. But the
women in these two "advertisements" had very different experiences. And only one — the snuff film — makes inequality
sexy.

These differences matter in the real world. In the real world,
real women are seen as pornography. Thus they cannot rise
above what men think they really are and what men will continue
to think they are, especially if the "fictions" of pornography
(which are advertised as the real thing, and which real men
seldom see as fictions) give men sexual pleasure. When June
Callwood dismisses the "puerile maunderings" of engineers[16] or
even the puerile maunderings of pornographers, she makes it
seem as if these maunderings do not really make any difference.
But if women are consistently reduced, dehumanized and objec-
tified through pornography, and if so much mass media, as
Kostash agrees, imitates those pornographic conventions, if

women are seen as sex, and sex only, how can women ever achieve equality? Will a man who loves pornography give a woman a raise if all he sees when he looks at her is a set of sex organs? Will he give her a raise if turning her down gives him an erotic charge? These questions are important.

Violence against women, in the form of sexual assault, incest, wife assault and sexual harassment, is systematic. The fact that these things happen has been well documented, even by men.[17] In addition, women have to confront pornography and its imitators every day. Thus pornography serves as a form of public terrorism. Because there is such a strong connection between pornography and violence against women, Anna Gronau treats pornography as "public proof that violence against women continues to exist in society."[18] But censorship, she argues, "removes the evidence."

I miss women's real experience in this analysis. Do women need pornography to prove the existence of violence against women? What about what women say about their own lives? What about what women know? Admittedly, women are often not believed, but that, I would contend, has something to do with the pervasiveness of pornography, for pornography tells lies about what women want and need sexually, lies which tend to be believed more than what real women say.[19] And that is the second flaw in Anna Gronau's analysis. She thinks that pornographic products are seen as documents of sexual oppression. It does not work that way. The "smile-bitch-or-I'll-kill-you" process of making pornography has a lot to do with what is believed and what is not believed. If Anna Gronau wants to know why pornography is not treated as "evidence," she could contact her associate Sara Diamond, who in the same book does everything she can to explain why what is going on in the pictures is not real. To Sara Diamond, pornography is only fantasy, or symbol, or image, or movie magic.[20]

"[C]ensoring pornography," writes Lynn King, "is like using an aspirin to cure cancer: it might ease the pain, but does not eliminate the disease, and may well have serious side effects."[21] I have never heard of a legal remedy that was intended to be the *sole* solution to social problems, or that would have much impact if there were no corresponding changes in perceptions or values. Why do we make these special demands of pornography law? We do not make similar demands of sexual assault laws. We know that rapists tend to commit rape more than once. Thus, keeping rapists off the street during the time of incarceration means that perhaps one or two random women (or maybe not so random, given the high incidence of spousal rape) will be spared. Most feminists know better than to imagine that by themselves, sexual assault laws will eliminate rape. Most feminists know that at best, those laws remind men, in spite of the cultural messages they may receive to the contrary, that if they commit this crime, something might happen to them. Varda Burstyn's utopian contention that we should ground legal and social actions in "the best of what people are living today and not the worst" misconstrues the point of legal remedies. Legal remedies exist to redress or avert harms.[22]

Women Against Censorship argue fairly consistently that most legal tools that are placed in the hands of the state will be used to hurt dissidents, radicals or anyone who is committed to social change. This is an abstract argument that does not resonate with reality. For example, a federal court recently decided that the Customs Tariff Act violates the Charter of Rights and Freedoms.[23] The Customs Tariff Act made it illegal to import immoral or indecent materials.[24] On an intellectual level, I think the decision is a good one, since the words *immoral* and *indecent* are meaningful to right-wing people and meaningless to feminists who understand that pornography is an issue of equality, power and wealth. But as a practical matter, the decision could have the devastating effect of flooding Canada with pornographic materials. I cannot believe that *Women Against Censorship* think that this practical result is a good thing.

As well, do *Women Against Censorship* imagine that the government will not fill this power vacuum? The polls in this country show that a majority of Canadians currently favour controls over pornography; our political culture fosters and supports government regulation; the Fraser Committee has published a report that not only confirms these trends, but also makes numerous suggestions on the kind of regulations that could be enacted; Canada is under the political sway of the Progressive Conservative Party. I think we can be almost certain that the Progressive Conservatives will find a way to enact legislation that will withstand a Charter challenge. I think that when they do, feminists should do everything they can to make sure that the new legislation reflects feminist concerns. My fear is that if feminists withdraw entirely from the legislative and legal process, there is an even *greater* risk that the *law* will be used against us.

Still, it is important to remember that present laws are used against dissidents and women. Mariana Valverde and Lorna Weir accurately describe how obscenity legislation has been used regularly against gay publications.[25] The Ontario Theatres Act, especially as amended by the proposed Bill 82, is an arrogant piece of legislation which refuses to take context and purpose into account in the censorship process. I do not deny that these abuses and excesses are real. But the existence of these excesses does *not* mean that lesbian and feminist material is "the first to go." The amount of imported pornographic material on the cutting room floor of the Theatres Branch is exponentially greater than the few frames of feminist artistic material that is eliminated by the censor board.[26]

In the midst of these assaults on obscenity doctrine, customs regulations and censor boards, comes "False Promises," which attacks the Dworkin-MacKinnon authored Minneapolis Ordinance.[27] I think there was some poor editorial judgement used here. Treating this ordinance as a subject for scrutiny in a book that attacks conventional forms of censorship makes it seem as if the ordinance is just another version of familiar formulas. It is not.[28]

The Minneapolis Ordinance treats pornography as sex discrimination and as a violation of women's civil rights, and it empowers women to sue pornographers in their own name for the damages caused to them through the practices of pornography. Community standards, which fluctuate within sexist and heterosexist parameters and which are relevant to obscenity law and censorship regulations, play no role in establishing liability. Only one standard applies, and it is a fixed standard: the standard of equality between the sexes. Police, who are poorly situated to determine the harm done by pornography,[29] play no role in the enforcement process of the ordinance, for it is a civil provision, not a criminal provision. Prior restraint plays no role in the enforcement process, unless an actual injury has been caused in the process of making a specific piece of pornographic material. The ordinance does recognize that law can be a vehicle for social change, and it gives women a voice in court. If this ordinance were put into effect, women would be able to argue that pornography sexually subordinates them, and they would be able to initiate legal action to redress the harm that it does to individuals.

Lisa Duggan and her co-authors complain that the ordinance will not eliminate sexism. As I have explained, legal remedies seldom can change sexual conditions of their own weight and without a political process occurring at the same time. They also complain that the ordinance does not restrict the definition of pornography to violent materials. They do not seem to understand that it never was intended to be so restricted. It was designed to address sexual subordination, not violence. Their main argument, though, is that the right wing will use the ordinance against progressive sexually explicit materials, especially against gay materials. Legally speaking, I am not certain I understand how this could happen. The courts have been extremely reluctant to recognize anything that happens between members of the same sex as sex discrimination. Before sex discrimination even becomes visible to the law, the law needs to see the presence of a gender/male and gender/female dynamic. I suppose one way a conservative female moralist might use the ordinance against gay male pornography would be to argue that she is sexually subordinated by sexually explicit materials which present subordinated gay males as female; merely saying they offend her will not work. But I do not think that right-wing women are prepared to do this, to use this kind of vocabulary or to take a feminist stance in court.

Politically speaking, this fear of right-wing abuse is what I call "future tense panic." Future tense panic leads people to confuse the present with the possible. At the present time, women are sexually subordinated in and by pornography. It is possible that the right wing will be able to co-opt this feminist strategy. In the Canadian context, I think this is such a small possibility that I am tempted to call the argument a manipulative scare tactic. The co-optive potential of the ordinance is a much smaller present threat to feminists than are the present powers of the police or of the film censors. Furthermore, the right wing in Canada is not embracing the strategy at all. Canadian moral majoratists trust the police far more than they trust women. Thus, they are more interested in strengthening police powers than they are in giving women the right to be active agents in the legal system. My concern is that if Canadian women discard a legal approach that empowers women, we run the risk of having the right wing write more repressive rules. Worse, we lose the opportunity to give a voice in court to those women who are used and used up in the oppressive practices of pornography.

Lynn King and June Callwood contend that the state is an enemy of feminism and that civil liberties and feminism form a good partnership. This is a sound viewpoint if feminism is defined as the activities of feminists who voice dissent, but the viewpoint loses something if feminism is defined as a politic that emerges from the real experience of women in general. I glossed over this point in my discussion of legal remedies, but the point is strengthened further if we consider civil liberties, their attendant right to privacy and what value they hold for women. Many women, after all, do not crave privacy. They dread it. Most of the violence against women takes place in private — in the family — where men's liberties, including their right to abuse women, remain, for all practical purposes, protected against any threat from state authority.[30] Women are beginning to sense that it is men's privacy that is at stake in the civil libertarian's worldview (at least as it gets acted out in real life), and that it is men whose individual freedoms are likely to remain intact if the civil libertarian's universe continues to unfold as it has.

More central to the pornography debate, however, is the civil libertarian's insistence that the state should not interfere with the distribution of ideas, for art and education are fundamental to the health of the body politic. But pornography is not an idea; pornography is a practice. Pornography is more act than art.

Pornography consists of concrete actions and physical responses. The only way to understand pornography as an abstraction is to imagine that an erection is only an idea, a premise that anyone who has ever apprehended an erection (to keep this discussion grounded in reality) ought to find difficult to accept.

However, the principle of freedom of expression remains central to feminist artists who want to articulate an alternative erotic vision. This "cultural offensive," as Lorna Weir and Mariana Valverde call it, is extremely important to the process of discovering alternatives to pornography. I do not think, however, that women's prose, poetry, eight millimeter films and video tapes by themselves will be able to counteract the effect of an industry that has more outlets than McDonald's. In fact, in a society in which money buys speech, feminist dissidents are allowed a few inroads, but the real beneficiaries of the civil liberties movement are the pornographers. And the pornographers will naturally champion civil liberties so that they can continue to silence women by convincing consumers that women have nothing to say in the first place.

Freedom of speech, a phrase used most often to subvert women's opposition to pornography, *does* mean something — to men. When men speak, people listen. When men speak, they are believed. Women, on the other hand, are silent. Women's credibility has been terribly damaged, both by the practices of pornographers who do have unlimited access to speech, and by the relentless promulgation of the liberal fiction that women share that unlimited access. As a result, even women's silence has been thoroughly distorted. What happens when women's voices are not heard? Is it mere coincidence that our silence is interpreted as consent? How does an absence of speech — an inability to speak — come to be interpreted as consent? Who makes this interpretation, and who benefits from it? To what extent has the wishful thinking of a civil liberties politic made certain that women's silence will be construed as freely chosen silence instead of as speech insidiously suppressed?

The commitment to civil liberties expressed by some of the writers in *Women Against Censorship* makes me appreciate the fact that the book was not called *Feminists Against Censorship*, even if that decision was made only for marketing reasons. I do wish though, that the book had been called *Women Against State Censorship*, because that is what it is about. It makes a number of arguments about how state censorship is the worst possible form of social and political control. I am not sure that the assessment would ring true for most women. I agree instead with Catharine MacKinnon's tidy formulation the "Feminism has no theory of the state. It has a theory of power."[31] Feminism needs a theory of power, because in a society that is defined by gender hierarchy, the experience of powerlessness is real for women. Men have power, and men are everywhere, and therefore power is situated in many different places. From a woman's standpoint, power is not necessarily more egregious when exercised by the state than it is when exercised by, say, a sexist editor who controls the means of media production, or much worse, by a battering husband.

The same is not true for privileged white middle-class males whose experience tells *them* that the only threat to their pursuit of happiness is state intrusion. To the privileged man who laments that the state has prevented him from seeing eight seconds of *The Tin Drum*,[32] I am tempted to say, "Feel grateful that this is the worst thing that could happen to you." And it is. He does not have to censor his movements or feel immobilized at night for fear of rape. He does not feel censored by culture itself: he does not cast his eye over an array of cultural products that hardly ever resonate with his own spirit, or he would not miss those eight seconds of commercial movie so badly. He will argue that state censorship is especially grim, backed up as it is by prison sentences and police powers. He would not understand that from a woman's view, there is no significant difference between being jailed by the warden or being incarcerated by an assaultive husband.

Varda Burstyn misses this point entirely.[33] She argues against state sanctions and supports instead any initiative that might put a dent in pornography sales and distribution. She reminds readers that a community telephone campaign that targeted pornography sold by Boots Drugstores was so successful that Boots proclaimed itself a "family store" and pulled all the "adult magazines" from the shelves. This, according to Burstyn, was a victory. But really, which is more dangerous for women: eliminating rape myth scenarios from films, scenes in which women are depicted as getting sexual pleasure from rape, in the name of state authority, or eliminating adult magazines from a drugstore, in the name of the family? Which has really been more dangerous for women — the family or the state? Which has been the more effective locus of male power? Under the aegis of which institution has most of the abuse of women taken place?

This is something about which women, and feminists, are deeply conflicted. No police swept into Boots. No charges were laid. The store got rid of the pornography. The family was celebrated. Did women win? Putting the dilemma another way, a woman walks alone down the street of a tough neighbourhood at night. She sees a police car. Does she feel as if her right to a private stroll has been violated, or does she feel safer? These are the questions feminists must begin to ask. *Women Against Censorship* did not ask those questions, apart from Anna Gronau's confession that she feels conflict between her identities as woman/victim and woman/artist. Instead, *Women Against Censorship* provide a conventional defense of civil liberties and a variation on marxist theory in which "men" are substituted for the ruling class. They completely ignore the emerging feminist perception that the relationship between women and the state is much more ambivalent than a civil liberties or marxist approach could ever allow.

The reason why the pornography debate has exasperated so many thoughtful women, and eluded so many others — including *Women Against Censorship* — is that the issue totally redesigns political debates that used to be very clear cut. This was illustrated splendidly last December, when police laid charges against *Penthouse* magazine.[34] In its attempt to contest the charges, Curtis Circulation, the company that distributes *Penthouse*, proceeded to purchase a full-page advertizement in the *Globe and Mail*, warning of the dangers of state intrusion and comparing the police action to Nazi bookburnings. When I read the advertizement, I knew that this was all wrong; that the old formulas would not work; that it was difficult to think of

Penthouse as a beleaguered dissident struggling against authority; that *Penthouse* was a propaganda machine that would impress even Joseph Goebbels; that from what women are saying about what has happened to them in the practices of pornography, the state is *not* to the pornographer what Nazis were to Jews and dissidents. It makes more sense the other way around: Nazis are to Jews what pornographers are to women. I think Andrea Dworkin explained best how pornography has transformed political discourse. "Pornographers," she writes, "are the secret police of male supremacy."[35]

But just as pornography is invisible in *Women Against Censorship*, so are the pornographers. Varda Burstyn tries to pick up some of the slack in her closing essay. "Beyond Despair" is a moving feminist document, and it is a valuable addition to the discussion of what to do about the way patriarchal structures and values have defined sexuality. She has made a serious attempt to integrate radical feminist perspectives with her own socialist feminist views; the result is a veritable blueprint for a feminist revolution, with strategies that include everything from sex education[36] to full employment. But these strategies do not touch the pornographers. Even the direct actions against "grossly sexist spectacles," as Varda Burstyn calls them, are intended to educate and not to shut them down. This is consistent with the general trend in the book, which is to view pornography as relatively benign. In the end, the future tense panic that characterizes *Women Against Censorship*'s opposition to the Minneapolis Ordinance has its analogue in the strategies that Varda Burstyn sets out. These strategies address the values of the next generation. They do not address the present tense oppression. The women who know that the pornography in their lives has something to do with the violence they experience deserve better. And the pornographers who have turned sexual abuse into an erotic spectacle deserve worse.

When I read *Women Against Censorship*, I could not push the sound of laughter out of my head. It was a pornographer laughing. And the women who have heard that sound, the women who do not speak in this book, know what that laughter augurs: their pain and sorrow, and ultimately the pain and sorrow of all women. I think we have to make it so that no woman has to hear that laughter, ever again.[37]

I would like to acknowledge the following women, whose work and encouragement has assisted me in developing my analysis of pornography: Leslie Chud, Brettel Dawson, Andrea Dworkin, Mary Lou Fassel, Lisa Freedman, Carole Geller, Connie Guberman, Catharine MacKinnon, Sheilah McIntyre, Nicole Tellier, Cindy Wilkie, Wendy Wine, Eve Zaremba and the members of the *Broadside* collective. I would also like to acknowledge the assistance I have received from The Canada Council, The Ontario Women's Directorate and The Women's Resource Centre at OISE.

NOTES

1. "We all see it as a gross dehumanization of women and we all know that whenever one group in society — in this case, men — convinces itself that another group is a subspecies, it becomes permissible to inflict suffering on the inferiors." June Callwood, "Feminist Debates and Civil Liberties," 122.

2. I have decided to ignore the grammatical convention that treats a book as a single (inanimate) object. Instead, I am using plural (feminine) referents in order to emphasize that the book is a medium for human voices.

3. For example, Sara Diamond, "Pornography: Image and Reality," 47. This is completely inconsistent with June Callwood's comments in note 1 above. June Callwood believes in civil liberties, yet Mariana Valverde and Lorna Weir comment: "At the same time a liberal approach that promises us moral support in case of unusual persecution is not very helpful either. Lesbians have few if any bookstores to be raided or defended: For us freedom of speech is not an existing freedom to be defended but a goal to work toward." Mariana Valverde and Lorna Weir, "Thrills, Chills and the 'Lesbian Threat' or, The Media, the State and Women's Sexuality," 105.

4. Lisa Steele, "A Capital Idea: Gendering in the Mass Media," 58-78.

5. This is not to say that men are not subordinated in pornography. In fact, young gay males who leave home in order to escape homophobia find themselves on city streets where they quickly learn that hustling is a way to survive. Still, I refer to subordination of women as a part of the definition of pornography because even when men are being subordinated, they are being treated like women.

6. Many women testified to this kind of experience at public hearings held by the Minneapolis City Council when it first contemplated adopting the sex discrimination ordinance. However, Linda Marchiano's life as Linda Lovelace has become a classic case. Linda Lovelace was the star of *Deep Throat*, which was the single most successful commercial pornographic film. It is about a woman whose clitoris is located in her throat. In a recent autobiography, Linda Marchiano describes how she was pimped, pushed around and forced to perform during the filming of *Deep Throat*. See Linda Marchiano, *Ordeal*, with Michael O'Brady (New Jersey: Citadel Press, 1980).

7. Women in shelters for assaulted women have described this kind of experience to me. The evidence is part of a survey of assaulted women, now in its beginning stages, to determine whether there is a connection between the violence these women have experienced and the pornography in their lives.

8. Carole Vance, Lisa Duggan and Nan Hunter, "False Promises: Feminist Antipornography Legislation in the U.S.," 130-151. Carole Vance and her co-authors also suggest that sexual pluralism must exist because they have some confidence in the values of liberal democracy. They do not take into account the way in which pornography helps to fuse the social meaning of *female* with submission and the social meaning of *male* as domination. Vance and her co-authors believe that we have sexual choice. But when I look at pornography, I do not see any evidence of the pluralism they are celebrating. To me, pornography looks much more like patriarchal sexual ideology, in which sexuality is gendered to the ground. I have discussed this at length in "Sexuality and Its Discontents," *Broadside* 6 (April 1985): 8-9.

Women Against Censorship seldom deal directly with the issue of sexuality. However, Varda Burstyn does posit that the only alternative to women's sexual liberation is Victorian repression. Varda Burstyn, "Political Precedents and Moral Crusades: Women, Sex and the State," 10-30. What about pornographic oppression? Sara Diamond hypothesizes that men use pornography and abuse sexuality because they are afraid of women; in their collective insecurity, they turn to pictures. She will not agree that men consume pornography because it feels good. Lisa Steele complains that anti-pornography activists think that pornography is a cankerous sore which has to be lanced (by state censorship) so that it will not kill the patient (society). Feminists who oppose pornography do not actually think this way. We think that pornography threatens women, not society, and we think that to keep women cowed and terrorized is absolutely consistent with society's sexist values and determination to keep all women in our/their place. Pornography is not a sore or a canker on society. It is the heartbeat of a sexist society — but it is not our hearts that beat according to the pornographer's scenarios, it is our sexuality.

9. Diamond, "Image and Reality," 47.

10. Myrna Kostash, "Second Thoughts," 32-39. I urge you to read Myrna Kostash, "Whose Body, Whose Self," in *Still Ain't Satisfied*, ed. Maureen Fitzgerald, Connie Guberman and Margie Wolfe (Toronto: Women's Press, 1982), 43-54. It is too bad that Myrna Kostash had second thoughts.

11. The "slippery slope" argument in the context of the debate over pornography points out that one small step toward interfering with civil liberties puts all of us on the slippery slope that leads to fascism, for if we surrender one liberty, we have no moral claim to any others. It is a version of an "all-or-nothing" argument.

12. Callwood, "Civil Liberties," 127.

13. "Snuff" films are advertised as showing the actual murder of women; this is meant to be the ultimate sexual turn-on. Although the original film (*Snuff*) was believed to be a hoax, the term still applies to the genre, and there is no evidence that snuff films do not actually exist.

14. Catharine A. MacKinnon, "Not a Moral Issue," *Yale Law and Policy Review* 2 (1984): 321.

15. Steele, "Mass Media," 77-78.

16. June Callwood is referring to the puerile maunderings of engineers at the University of Saskatchewan, whose publication (*The Red Eye*) contained materials which women at the school believed violated their human rights. See Saskatchewan Human Rights Commission v. Waldo (1984), 5 C.H.R.R. par. 17609-17783 (Bd. of Inquiry) (under appeal). The board agreed that the materials violated the rights of women on campus. June Callwood plainly disapproves of the decision and of the women who filed the complaint. Callwood, "Civil Liberties," 127.

17. In Canada, one out of four women are the survivors of incest. See Robin Badgely et al., "Report on Sexual Offenses Against Children," (Ottawa: Ministry of Supply and Services, 1984), 114. A woman is raped in Canada every seventeen minutes. See Julie Brickman, "Incidence of Rape and Sexual Assault in an Urban Canadian Population," *International Journal of Women's Studies* 7 (1984): 195-206. One out of ten women who live with a spouse is beaten by him. See Linda McLeod, *Wife Battering in Canada: The Vicious Circle* (Ottawa: Canadian Advisory Council on the Status of Women, 1980), 21. See also Diana Russell, *Sexual Exploitation* (Beverly Hills, Calif.: Sage Publications, 1984). Diana Russell, using wider definitions of sexual abuse — definitions that stem from women's descriptions of their real experiences — reports higher incidence. But generally, the more this kind of violence is studied, the greater the reported incidence.

18. Anna Gronau, "Women and Images: Toward a Feminist Analysis of Censorship," 91-98.

19. There are clinical studies that show this to be true. See especially James Check and Neil Malamuth, "The Effects of Mass Media Exposure on Acceptance Values of Violence Against Women: A Field Experiment," *Journal of Research in Personality* 15 (1981): 436-446. Any woman who has been told "Come on, you know you love it" by a persistent male can grasp this point.

20. Diamond, "Image and Reality," 46-49.

21. King, "Changing the Laws," 79.

22. Canada's criminal justice system is in itself discriminatory and deserves some sharp criticism. Women in conflict with the law usually commit crimes that will alleviate the circumstances of poverty that is feminized in a sexist society; prostitution law, among others, discriminates in this way. I do not think that all criminal laws should be repealed for this reason. Nor do I think that the sexual assault laws should be repealed because the process of seeing a complaint through to conviction is admittedly traumatic. Most of the legal analysis in *Women Against Censorship*, however, suggests that they should be repealed.

23. Luscher v. Deputy Minister, Revenue Canada, Customs and Excise (1985), 45 C.R. (3d) 81 (F.C.A.) per Thurlow C.J.F.C., Mahoney and Hugesson J.J.

24. Customs Tariff Act, R.S.C. 1970 ch. C-41, s. 14, Sched. C, item 99201-1.

25. Valverde and Weir, "Lesbian Threat," 99-103. This is because obscen-

ity convictions depend on an assessment of community standards, which are bound to be homophobic in a heterosexist society. Obscenity law has not only placed the products of gay culture in persistent peril, but it has also not done very much to curb the growth of the pornography industry. In a precedent-setting decision, Borins J. ruled that woman-degrading material was obscene, even though it did not depict explicit genital sexual activity. In this decision, Borins J. complained about having to apply so-called community standards when a judge is supposed to be distanced, impartial, and so on. See R. v. Doug Rankine Co. (1983), 36 C.R. (3d) 154, 9 C.C.C. (3d) 53 (Ont. Co. Ct.) per Borins Co. Ct. J. However, an Alberta judge recently ruled that a film which depicts homosexual acts between consenting adults is not obscene. This ruling suggests that judges might be able to see the difference between pornography and non-degrading erotica. See R. v. Wagner (1985), 43 C.R. (3d) 318, 36 Alta. L.R. (2d) 301 (Q.B.), per Shannon J. Both decisions have been cited with approval in R. v. Red Hot Video Ltd. (1985), 45 C.R. (3d) 36 (B.C.C.A.), per Nemetz C.J.B.C., Hinkson and Anderson JJ.A, and in Towne Cinema Theatres Ltd. v. R. (1985), 45 C.R. (3d) 1 (S.C.C.), per Dickson C.J.C., Beetz, Estey, McIntyre, Lamer, Wilson, and LeDain JJ. Note that even if the community standards approach were to be completely supplanted by a "feminist" concept of obscenity which looks to elements like dehumanization, degradation or consent, the Linda Marchiano situation is not affected, for judges look only at the pictures — not at the process by which they are made. See R. v. Ramsingh (1984), 14 C.C.C. (3d) 230 (Man. Q.B.) per Ferg J., who ruled that *Deep Throat* was not obscene because film depictions of consensual sexual acts are "acceptable." The deep irony in this line of "feminist" cases is that with the emphasis on issues of (apparent) consent and violence, it may be becoming *more* difficult (instead of easier) to oppose the distribution of pornography that is made under coercive and violent conditions.

26. See Susan Cole, "Combatting the Practice of Pornography," *Broadside* 5 (1984) 10: 6-7.

27. Duggan, Hunter and Vance, "False Promises: Feminist Antipornography Legislation in the U.S.," 130-151. The ordinance was proposed as an amendment to the Minneapolis Minnesota Code of Ordinances Relating to Civil Rights, tit. 7, chs. 139, 141, after extensive hearings on pornography were conducted in December 1983. The transcripts of those hearings offer compelling testimony about the harm that pornography causes. The city council passed the ordinance in December 1983; the mayor vetoed it in January 1984; the

city council passed it again in July 1984; the mayor vetoed it again. The Indianapolis City Council passed a similar ordinance in April 1984, as General Ordinance No. 24, amending the Indianapolis and Marion County, Indiana Code, ch. 16. The ordinance was then challenged on first amendment grounds by civil liberties groups and media trade groups; Judge Sara Evans Barker held that the ordinance was unconstitutional. See American Bookseller Ass. Inc. v. Hudnut, 598 F. Supp. 1316 (S.D. Ind. 1984), affirmed August 27, 1985 (CCA 7) per Cudahy, Easterbrook CJ and Swygert SCJ (docket no. 84-3147). Catharine MacKinnon has pointed out that Judge Sara Evans Barker is a conservative former prosecutor and was appointed to the bench by Ronald Reagan, and that Judge Easterbrook is also a Reagan appointee. If the alliance between right-wing conservatives and anti-pornography feminists is so inevitable — as anti-censorship feminists claim — then *why* are conservative Reagan appointed judges striking this law down?

28. For more on this, see Cole, "Combatting" and Mary Lou Fassel, "A Powerful Weapon," *Broadside* 6 (1985) 7: 9-10. Compare Reva Landau, "Flaws in the Law," *Broadside* 6 (1985) 7: 8. In contrast to these United States writers, Reva Landau thinks that if the ordinance were adapted to Canada, it would do too little, not too much. It is ironic that the authors of "False Promises" — women who call themselves feminists — should launch this attack on the authors of the ordinance, since Catharine MacKinnon has written the most comprehensive feminist critique of existing obscenity legislation, legislation that these authors also oppose. While many observers have claimed that pornography has brought together unusual groups (like feminists and conservatives), it is just as intriguing to note that the pornography issue has also torn apart otherwise solid alliances.

29. This statement is not just a rhetorical flourish. I attended a police academy in Aylmer, Ontario to observe how police officers are trained to enforce obscenity legislation. There were about forty officers in the class. Before beginning the class, the lecturer asked how many of the students had ever seen "hardcore porn." All but two raised their hands. Since this was a training session, it was apparent that they had seen such material on their own time — not on the job.

30. "Why then has the demand for privacy centred so exclusively on preserving the traditional domain of male privilege? And why do the staunchest defenders of that view fail to see that in invoking these principles within a domain characterized by fundamental sexual inequality they are in fact reinforcing that inequality and sanctioning its

worst abuses?" Lorenne Clark, "Liberalism and Pornography," in *Pornography and Censorship*, ed. Copp Wendell (Buffalo, New York: Prometheus, 1983), 50.

31. Catharine A. MacKinnon, "Feminism, Marxism, Method and the State: Toward a Feminist Jurisprudence," *Signs* 8 (1983): 635.

32. The refusal to give *The Tin Drum* a public screening was I think one of the board's mistakes, and it severely detracted from the board's credibility. The sequence that was cut depicted the protagonist as a young boy going under a woman's skirts. The scene was not sexually explicit and the character was played by an adult dwarf.

33. Varda Burstyn, "Beyond Despair: Positive Strategies," 152-180.

34. The December issue of *Penthouse* featured Sakura-style photographs of nude Japanese women bound tightly hanging from trees and buildings. When customs officials were questioned about admitting the materials into the country, they said that the violence was merely implied. Regina v. Metro News Limited, unreported (Ont. D.C.) per Sheard J. (under appeal), ruled that the materials were obscene.

35. Andrea Dworkin, "Against the Male Flood: Censorship, Pornography and Equality," *Harvard Women's Law Journal* 8 (1985): 13. I should add that until feminists have more comprehensive information based on women's real experiences, and not on masculinist theories, it is a mistake for women to say that we really know what to think about censorship. We should confess our ambivalence. My way of doing it is to refer to myself as a feminist who is not anti-censorship (eschewing a pro-censorship label), thereby making sure that I am placed in such a way so as not to have discarded a single remedy that might improve the condition of women.

36. Varda Burstyn's discussion of sex education is the best I have read on the subject, and the other strategies do indicate that she is interested in new approaches to rights and the law. For example, she suggests that women who have pornography forced upon them in places of work should deal with it through sexual harassment complaints. Burstyn, "Beyond Despair," 159. But again, these solutions let pornographers off the hook.

37. As this review goes to press, I suspect that *Penthouse* publisher Bob Guccione is laughing the loudest. I notice that *Forum* has published an interview with Varda Burstyn, complete with a full-page picture. See Philip Nobile, "An Interview with Varda Burstyn," *Forum* (September 1985): 12-17, 58. The article ostensibly promotes *Women Against Censorship. Forum* is Bob Guccione's quasi-sexology por-

nography magazine; it takes its theme from the *Penthouse* feature "Forum," which invites readers to submit stories of their own sexual experiences for publication. The ease with which feminist anti-censorship arguments (not to mention anti-censorship feminists themselves) can be appropriated by pornographers is altogether too plain here. And the possibility that anti-pornography feminists might some day play into the hands of the religious right is more speculative and not nearly as chilling as the fact that anti-censorship feminists are *already* in the hands of the pornographers.

NOTES

CHAPTER I: PORNOGRAPHY

1. This idea was first promoted by Andrea Dworkin in *Pornography: Men Possessing Women* (New York: Perogee, 1981), and by Catharine A. MacKinnon in "Francis Biddle's Sister," in *Feminism Unmodifed: Discourses on Life and Law* (Cambridge: Harvard University Press, 1987). The two have recently co-authored *Pornography and Civil Rights: A New Day for Women's Equality* (Minneapolis: Organizing Against Pornography, 1988).

2. Linda Lovelace, *Ordeal* (New York: Citadel, 1980). Throughout my own text, Linda Lovelace will be referred to by her real name, Linda Marchiano, out of respect for her desire to put away her past and any connections she had with the pornography industry.

3. "Five officials who scan porn rule what enters country," *Toronto Star*, 20 November 1984. "The difficulty with the *Penthouse* editorial is that the violence is implied, not explicit," according to Customs official Tom Greig. See also Regina v. Metro News Limited, unreported (Ont. D.C.) per Sheard J., in which the materials were deemed obscene. The decision was unusual in that it identified the materials as obscene even though there was not, legally speaking, any sexual explicitness. This kind of so-called feminist decision in obscenity cases is discussed in depth in Chapter II.

4. According to the *Oxford Dictionary*, a "pornograph" is defined as an "obscene writing or pictorial illustration." I am resurrecting the word, not the definition.

5. Carol Gilligan's intriguing study *In an Different Voice: Psychological Theory and Women's Development* (Cambridge: Harvard University Press, 1982) describes how males tend to view moral dilemmas in terms of right and wrong, while females tend to view them as problems that can be solved through human interaction. I call the male tendency the masculinist aversion to ambiguity.

6. Dworkin, "Against the Male Flood," *Harvard Women's Law Journal* 8 (1985).

7. This term was coined by researchers James Check and Neil Malamuth, whose groundbreaking studies will be discussed later, and by Wendy Stock, who applied their research strategy to women.

8. Vanessa Williams described how after publication of the photos she "had hit rock bottom," in *People*, 6 August 1984, 81. Gloria Steinem described the experience of being humiliated by *Screw* in *Outrageous Acts and Everyday Rebellions* (New York: Holt Reinhart and Winston, 1983), 23.

9. The studio was not typical in that it was operated by a woman, but the rates were typical. In 1984, Suze Randall was paying models $300 a session. I've increased the figure to keep up with inflation.

10. Artistic or literary merit is often one of these redeeming social values. See Regina v. Odeon Morton Theatres (1974) 16 C.C.C. (2d) 185.

11. This is almost exactly Margaret Baldwin's language in "The Sexuality of Inequality: The Minneapolis Pornography Ordinance," *Journal of Law and Inequality* (1984): 629.

12. See Mariana Valverde, "The White Imperialist Gaze," *Broadside*, vol. 7 no. 9 (July 1986).

13. Rush, Florence. *The Best Kept Secret: Sexual Abuse of Children*. (Englewood Cliffs, N.J.: Prentice-Hall, 1980).

14. Varda Burstyn makes this comment in "Art and Censorship," *Fuse* (Fall 1983).

15. Griselda Pollack and Rozsika Parker's *Old Mistresses: Women, Art and Ideology* (London: Routledge and Kegan Paul, 1981) has been extremely useful in the development of these ideas on art institutions. See also John Berger, *Ways of Seeing* (London: BBC, 1982) for expositions on such interesting statements as "She is not naked as she is, she is naked as the spectator sees." (50).

16. See Dworkin, *Pornography: Men Possessing Women*.

17. Kerri Kwinter's article "The Fashioned Face," *Fuse* (March 1980) was useful here.

18. This is a variation on a comment made by Catharine MacKinnon at the Women at the Law Conference in New York, 1986. "No pornographer has any trouble knowing what to make; no adult bookstore or theatre has any trouble knowing what to stock; no consumer has any trouble knowing what to buy."

19. Sara Diamond's essay in Varda Burstyn, ed., *Women Against Censorship* (Vancouver: Douglas & McIntyre, 1985), entitled "Pornography:

Image and Reality," is laced with these terms and the insistence that what we see in pornography is not real.

20. This unpublished study was undertaken by myself with the assistance of the Ontario Women's Directorate. Women staying at shelters in Ontario were surveyed and asked five questions: Does your partner use pornography and if so, what kind? Does he ask, expect or force you to buy it? Does he ask, expect or force you to use it? Does he ask expect or force you to replicate the activities in the pictures? How does this make you feel?

21. Diana E.H. Russell, *Sexual Exploitation: Rape, Child Sexual Abuse, and Workplace Harassment*, (Beverly Hills: Sage, 1984).

22. In public lectures, I have asked incredulous men to replicate these poses so that they can understand what former *Playboy* pin-up Deborah Shelton meant when she made this statement.

23. In the shelter study (see note 20 above), of the 105 women surveyed, 24 per cent of the women whose spouses used pornography were forced to buy the materials, representing 13 per cent of the entire sample. 25 per cent of the women whose spouses used pornography were forced to look at it. Further, a full 48 per cent of the women whose spouses used pornography, representing 25 per cent of the entire sample, reported having to replicate the activities in the pictures against their will. All of the women described these experiences as dehumanizing in some way.

24. Herceg v. *Hustler* Magazine Inc., (1983, SC Texas) 565 F. Supp. 802.

25. The figure was calculated by Catharine MacKinnon based on Diana Russell's data.

26. I'll stand by this position even though Diana Russell has written a persuasive paper contending that pornography causes harm. "Pornography and Rape: A Causal Model," *Political Psychology* vol. 9 no. 1 (March 1988).

27. L. Baron and M. Straus, "Sexual stratification, Pornography and Rape," in Ed Donnerstein and Neil M. Malamuth, eds., *Pornography and Aggression* (New York: Academic, 1984).

28. James V.P. Check, "A survey of Canadians' Attitudes Regarding Sexual Content in the Media," undertaken through the Lamarsh Research Program at York University (unpublished). 1985.

29. Malamuth and Check, "Penile tumescence and perceptual response to rape as a function of victim's preceived reactions," *Journal of Applied Social Psychology* vol. 10 no. 6: 528-554. The questionnaire

administered to subjects contained questions of a true/false nature, like "A woman who hitchhikes deserves to be raped," or "A woman who dresses scantily is asking for it." See also Malamuth et al., "Testing hypotheses regarding rape, exposures to sexual violence, sex difference and the normality of rapists," *Journal of Research in Personality*, vol. 14 (1980): 121-137; and Malamuth and Check, "The effects of mass media exposure on acceptance of violence against women: a field experiment," *Journal of Research in Personality*, vol. 15 (1981): 436-446.

It's interesting to track the results of similar studies performed on women. See Wendy Stock, "The effects of pornography on women," invited testimony for the Attorney General's Commission on Pornography, third hearing, September 11 and 12, 1985, Houston, Texas. Stock discovered that exposure to rape myths increased women's sexual arousal to rape and increased their rape fantasies. It did *not*, however, convince them that women liked force in sex.

30. At the Women and the Law conference held in Chicago in 1987, Valerie Heller gave moving testimony to the way her experience as an incest victim was lived out again and again in pornography abuse.

31. This research and the work that preceded it is described in Ed Donnerstein, "Pornography: its effect on violence against women," in *Pornography and Sexual Aggression*, 115-138. See also Daniel Linz, "Sexual violence in mass media: effects on male viewers and implications for society," University of Wisconsin, unpublished (1985). While the study results have been very useful, it is fascinating to note what male researchers do to find harm in pornography. They show violent pornography to male subjects, wiring up their brains, their hearts or their penises to see what effect the materials have on *them*, when the violence done to the women in pornography is right in front of their eyes on the screen.

32. In Donnerstein's study (see note 31 above), he took his subjects to participate in a mock rape trial held at the university law school. The subjects heard testimony from a woman who had been raped and were asked to assess her evidence and pass sentence on the perpetrator. The subjects trivialized the woman's injuries significantly more than a control group which had not seen the films, and passed a significantly lighter sentence than the control group. The results indicate that prolonged viewing of violent pornography has effects that cross over into real life situations. I think that the studies also show that the as long as violent pornography is a mass media staple, we will have a hard time getting people to take sexual assault seriously.

As Wendy Stock did with the Malamuth/Check research program, Carol Krafka applied the Donnerstein/Linz strategy to women. She discovered that like the male subject group, her female subjects grew less upset with the violence the more they saw, and that they rated the materials less violent the more they saw. But these women did *not* trivialize a rape victim's injuries at the mock trial. C.L. Krafka, "Sexually explicit, sexually violent and violent media: the effects of multiple naturalistic exposure and debriefing on female viewers." University of Wisconsin, unpublished (1985). In both Stock's and Krafka's studies on women, the materials *did* affect the women adversely, but it did not change their *attitudes* about sexual assault. Perhaps this is because many of them know what it feels like to be victimized.

33. Dolf Zillman and Jennings Bryant, "Effects of massive exposure to pornography," in *Pornography and Sexual Aggression*, 115-138.

34. This view has been expressed in many places, especially wherever the feminist anti-pornography movement is referred to as a moral panic. See, for example, Varda Burstyn, "Political Precedents and Moral Crusades: Women, Sex and the State" in Burstyn, ed., *Women Against Censorship* (Vancouver: Douglas & McIntyre, 1985); and the afterword in Judith Walkowitz, *Prostitution and Victorian Society: Women, Class and the State*. (Cambridge: Cambridge University Press, 1980).

35. "We're family people," said Nancy Pollack, the president of Canadians for Decency, in an interview with me.

36. For an excellent analysis of why right-wing women think the way they do, see Dworkin, *Right Wing Women* (New York: Perigee, 1982). If you have never read any of Dworkin's awesome work, I think this is the book to read. Dworkin is, in my opinion, the most talked about and under-read writer in the U.S.

37. "Lust keeps us in chains," said Nancy Pollack in the interview noted above.

38. These words were written in a letter from Jancis Andrews to British Columbia Ombudsman Ruth Lawrence-Campbell in the fall of 1982, dated December 23, 1982.

39. Jancis Andrews wrote this to me, January 2, 1984, in response to my request for information about the North Vancouver Women's Centre's organization against pornography.

40. See the appendix for a review of *Women Against Censorship*.

41. The term sex liberals will be examined in depth in Chapter III. For

the moment, it has the same meaning as sex libertarians.

42. In her speech to the Women and the Law conference in New York (note 18 above), Catharine MacKinnon said, "the more money you have the more speech you can buy."

43. MacKinnon's work, cutting through the traditional dichotomies of right and left, immoral and moral, makes her one of the most important feminist thinkers. "Obscenity is a moral idea; pornography is a political practice," she writes in her article "Not a Moral Issue" in *Feminism Unmodifed*. There she makes the distinction between feminist politics and right-wing moralism. See also Lorenne Clark's excellent article "Liberalism and Pornography," in D. Copp, and S. Wendell, eds., *Pornography and Censorship* (New York: Prometheus, 1983). Clark writes, "Why then has the demand for privacy centred so exclusively on preserving the traditional domain of male privilege? And why do the staunchest defenders of that view fail to see that in invoking these principles within a domain characterized by fundamental inequality they are in fact reinforcing that inequality and sanctioning its worst abuses?"

CHAPTER II: THE LAW

1. Some of this material appeared in a report prepared for the Ontario Women's Directorate on behalf of the Civil Rights and Remedies Committee, Toronto, 1987.

2. There is a lengthy American case law to illustrate this syndrome. See, for example, Cohen v. California, 403 U.S. 15, 25 (1970) (Harlan, J.) ("One man's vulgarity is another man's lyric."); Winters v. New York, 333 U.S. 507, 510 (1947) ("What is one man's amusement, teaches another's doctrine."), etc. Catharine MacKinnon refers to this catalogue of commentaries as the "one man's this is another man's that" doctrine. "Francis Biddle's Sister," in *Feminism Unmodified: Discourses on Life and Law* (Cambridge: Harvard University Press, 1987).

3. MacKinnon and Dworkin describe the problem of looking at pornography as a concept, ideas or images this way: "Once pornography is framed as a concept rather than a practice, more thought than act, more in the head than in the world, its effects also necessarily appear both insubstantial and unsubstantiated, more abstract than real." *Pornography and Civil Rights: A New Day for*

Women's Equality (Minneapolis: Organizing Against Pornography, 1988).

4. California Federal Savings and Loan Association et al. v. Gurra, Director, Department of Fair Employment and Housing et al. 93 L. Ed. 2d 613 (1987).

5. In fact, the Legal Education and Action Fund (LEAF) intervened in a case that determined that a gender-specific law could be tolerated under the Charter. See Schachter v. The Queen et al., decided June 7, 1988, Federal Court (Trial Division), per Barry Strayer J. The case involved maintaining longer maternity leaves than paternity leaves.

6. I attended a training session at the Provincial Police Academy in Aylmer, Ontario, in which officers were learning how to implement obscenity law. None of the thirty or so officers had been professionally active in the area and yet when the instructor asked how many of them had seen pornography, all but two put up their hands.

7. R. v. Curl, 2 Strange 788 E.R. 849 (K.B. 1727).

8. Ibid.

9. R. v. Hicklin L.R. 3 Q.B. 360 1868.

10. Voride v. The Queen (1962) S.C.R. 681 D.L.R. (3d) 507.

11. Criminal Code, 1892, 55-56 Vitc., c, 29 Section 179(c). In the U.S. People v. Byrne 99 Misc. 1 6 (N.Y. 1917), women were expressly forbidden from distributing birth control information because the materials were too sexually explicit.

12. See Criminal Code as in note 11 above.

13. Ibid.

14. See Gary Kinsman, *The Regulation of Desire: Sexuality in Canada.* (Montreal: Black Rose, 1987).

15. Regina v. Brodie (1962) 132 C.C.C. 161 and Dominion News and Gifts Ltd v. the Queen (1963) 2 C.C.C 103, 42 W.W.R. 65 (Man C.A.).

16. In Dominion News and Gifts, (note 15 above) at 116-117.

17. See Kinsman, note 14 above.

18. "It is apparent from a review of the case law that 'undue exploitation of sex' in the new definition came to be interpreted as nothing more than the degree of explicitness of sexual depiction." Kathleen E. Mahoney, "Obscenity, Morals and Law: A Feminist Critique," *Ottawa Law Review* 17:58. As far as I am concerned this is the best feminist survey of Canadian pornography law available.

19. Project P was established in 1975 in response to the rapid proliferation of so-called massage parlours on Toronto's Yonge Street. Its mandate is to investigate the distributors of pornography and to lay appropriate charges. In the course of its work, the Project has developed one of the most complete collections of pornography in the country, evidence of which can be seen in the presentations Project P makes to the public.

20. The encounter led me to write that it is absurd that it is illegal to depict a woman sucking a penis but perfectly legitimate to depict her sucking a gun. See Susan G. Cole, "Confronting Pornography: Bound, Gagged and Silenced," *Broadside* vol. 4, no. 10. (July-August 1983). Although the statement is often quoted by anti-censorship activists, I no longer hold the view that there is nothing problematic with pornographs presenting women in scenarios of fellatio.

21. R. v. Rankine Co., 35C.R. (3d) 154 9C.C.C. (3d) 53 (Ont. Cty. Ct.) 1983.

22. Ibid.

23. Ibid. In the same case, Judge Borins did uphold the precedents against sexual explicitness by deeming obscene sexually explicit videos that were not explicitly violent.

24. Ibid.

25. Catharine A. MacKinnon, "Not a Moral Issue," in *Feminism Unmodified*. "Pornography is not bad manners or a poor choice of audience, obscenity is."

26. The subject of R. v. Curl was *Venus in the Cloister or the Nun in her Smock*.

27. R. v. *Penthouse* (1979), 96 D.L.R. (3d), 735 (Ont. C.A).

28. R. v. Esther Bogyo and Marc Glassman, Ont. Prov. Court, Nov 26-27 1985. Judge Sidney Harris presiding (unreported).

29. R. v. Wagner (1985), 43 C.R. (3d) 318, 36 Alta L.R. (2d) 301 (Q.B.).

30. R. v. Ramsingh (1984) 14 C.C.C. (3d) 230 (Man. Q.B.).

31. Gloria Steinem, "Erotica Vs. Pornography," in *Outrageous Acts and Everyday Rebellions* (New York: Holt Reinhart & Winston, 1983).

32. Apparently drafters of the bill were struggling with the formulation and came to a consultation with feminists suggesting simply that scenarios of lactation and menstruation be included in the definition of pornography. Feminists explained that it wasn't lactation and menstruation per se that were problematic, but those scenarios in a sexual context. The phrase "in a sexual context" was used to qualify

a difference between educational materials and pornography. It was never meant as a legal term, and when "in a sexual context" appeared in the actual bill, the women involved in the consultation were appalled.

33. See R. v. Odeon Morton Theatres (1974) 16 C.C.C. (2d) 185 for a case that judges artistic merit as a defense for obscenity.

34. *Pornography and Prostitution in Canada: Report of the Special Committee on Pornography and Prostitution*, vol. I. (Ottawa: Minister of Supply and Services Canada, 1985), 160.

35. See Priape Enrg. et al. and the Deputy Minister of national Revenue (1980) 52 C.C.C. 2d 44 (Que. Sup. Ct.).

36. Re Luscher and Deputy Minister, Revenue Canada. 149 D.L.R. (3d) 243 (B.C. Cty. Ct. 1983).

37. See Helen Longino, "Pornography, Oppression and Freedom: A Closer Look," in Laura Lederer, ed., *Take Back the Night* (New York: William Morrow, 1980). This is considered the basic feminist text on pornography and includes over 30 articles on various aspects of of the subject.

38. This data comes from the Canadian Coalition Against Customs Censorship (CCACC), a group of activists who have kept meticulous records of customs seizures. As of this writing the most recent non-pornographic (non-gay) target of Canada Customs was Kathy Acker's *Empire of the Senseless* (New York: Grove, 1988), a harrowing fictional account of sexual abuse and the post-nuclear holocaust landscape. Acker describes herself as a feminist. The book is sexually explicit because of what it describes, not because of what it promotes.

39. *Patches* (July 1986).

40. Ontario Film and Video Appreciation Society and the Ontario Board of Censors, 41 O.R. (2d) 583. 1474 D.L.R. (3d) 58 (H.C.1983).

41. For a detailed description of the political and legal thinking behind this strategy, see Dworkin and MacKinnon, *Pornography and Civil Rights* (note 3 above). The ordinance was proposed as an amendment to the Minneapolis Minnesota Code of Ordinances Relating to Civil Rights, tit. 7, chs. 139, 141, after extensive hearings on pornography were conducted in December, 1983. The city council passed the ordinance in December, 1983; the mayor vetoed it in January, 1984; the city council passed it again in July, 1984; the mayor vetoed it again. The Indianapolis city council passed a similar ordinance in April, 1984, as General Ordinance No. 24, amending the Indianapolis and Marion County, Indiana Code, ch. 16. The ordinance was then

challenged on first amendment grounds by civil liberties groups and media trade groups; Judge Sara Evans Barker held that the ordinance was unconstitutional. See American Bookseller Ass. Inc. v. Hudnut, 598 F. Supp. 1316 (S.D. Ind. 1984), affirmed August 27, 1985 (CCA 7) per Cudahy, Easterbrook CJ and Swygert SCJ (docket no. 84-3147). The Minneapolis definition of pornography and five causes of action were placed in referendum on the presidential ballot, November 1988, in the city of Bellingham, Washington and passed. When the American Civil Liberties Union sued the city on first amendment grounds and the city refused to defend the law, Washington Women for Civil Rights intervened as partners. The case is pending.

42. "Public Hearings on Ordinances to Add Pornography as Discrimination Against Women," Committee on Government Operations, City Council, Minneapolis, Minn. Dec 12-13, 1983, on file with the *Harvard Civil Rights-Civil Liberties Law Review.*

CHAPTER III: THE SEX CRISIS

1. Susan Griffen, although she would not call herself a sex liberal, takes this position in her book *Pornography and Silence* (San Franscisco: Harper and Row, 1982).

2. See, for example, Lisa Steele's comment: "Sex is not the problem, sexism is," in "A Capital Idea," in Varda Burstyn, ed., *Women Against Censorship* (Vancouver: Douglas & McIntyre, 1985).

3. The *Village Voice* in New York and *NOW*, a Toronto news and entertainment weekly, both promote a leftist editorial stance while leaving their personals entirely uncensored.

4. See Catharine A. MacKinnon, "A Feminist/Political Approach," in James H. Gee and William T. O'Donohue, eds., *Theories of Human Sexuality* (New York: Plenum, 1987). "...it has become customary to affirm that sexuality is socially constructed. Seldom specified is what, socially, it is constructed *of*. When capitalism is the favoured social construct, sexuality is shaped and controlled and exploited and repressed by capitalism; not, capitalism creates sexuality as we know it. *Constructed* seems to mean influenced by, directed, channeled, like a highway constructs traffic patterns. Not: Why cars? Who's driving? Where's everybody going? What makes mobility matter? Who can own a car? Is there a pattern that makes these accidents look not very accidental?" (70).

5. Roszika Parker and Griselda Pollack develop this thesis in *Old Mistresses: Women, Art and Ideology* (London: Routledge and Kegan Paul, 1981).

6. See E. Ann Kaplan's feminist classic "Is the Gaze Male?" in E.A. Kaplan, ed., *Women and Film: Both Sides of the Camera* (New York: Methuen, 1983).

7. Sex manuals promote their so-called objective views on sex the way sex institutes like the Kinsey Institute promote their so-called objective sex research. I doubt the objectivity of their methods and their goals when a large portion of the research is made possible through grants from the Playboy Foundation.

8. Alexandra Penney, *Great Sex* (New York: Putnam, 1985), 102.

9. Mimi H. Silbert and Ayala M. Pines, "Early Sexual Exploitation as in Influence in Prostitution," *Social Work* (July-August 1983). There are a number of other important texts that shed a great deal of light on the prostitution issue. See Kathleen Barry, *Female Sexual Slavery* (New York: Prentice Hall, 1977). Also, K. Barry, C. Bunch and S. Castley, eds., *International Feminism: Networking Against Female Sexual Slavery* (New York: International Women's Tribute Centre, 1984).

Organized sex workers and their advocates have tried hard to silence these facts about prostitutes and the sexual abuse in their pasts. At a Toronto conference called Challenging Our Images, held in the fall of 1985, one prostitutes' rights organizer said flatly: "I want to dispel the myth that sexually abused women on the street are prostitutes because they are sexually abused. That is something academics use for their little statistics and their little studies. The kids I know on the street are running from sexual abuse, but they are not turning to prostitution because of sexual abuse, they are turning to prostitution because there are no social services available...Sexual abuse is only an indirect cause of women turning to prostitution."

This insistence that it is financial vulnerability only that drives women to prostitution is reminiscent of the way observers of wife assault used to say that women stayed in abusive relationships only because they could not afford to leave. Eventually, the fact that teenagers living with their parents were in assaultive relationships, even when there was no financial pressure to stay, forced a change in perspectives to include a discussion of the sexual and romantic dynamics of wife assault. In the same way, a discussion of the sexual dynamics, how it feels to have sex for pay, has to be included the discussion of prostitution.

10. Among the best in this vast literature are S. Butler, *Conspiracy of*

Silence (New York: Bantam, 1979); Diana E.H. Russell, *The Secret Trauma* (New York: Basic, 1986); and D. Finkelhor, *Child Sexual Abuse* (New York: Free Press, 1984).

11. See Russell, note 10 above.

12. See Paula J. Caplan, *The Myth of Women's Masochism* (New York: Signet, 1987) for an excellent discussion of the way what is perceived as women's masochism is constructed by women's social reality.

13. See Finkelhor, note 10 above.

14. See MacKinnon, note 4 above.

15. S. Head, S. Mercer and M. Hale, "A study of attitudes and behaviour in dating relationships with special reference to the use of of force among 417 Grade 13/OAC family studies students." Unpublished, prepared for the Scarborough Board of Education, June 1988.

16. Because Donnerstein failed to develop his own materials, he decided to use R-rated slasher films for his studies. This means that the findings he generated are less hypothetical than they might have been had he used new materials, for the results came out of studies on materials that were already in the local theatres in Madison, Wisconsin.

17. Adrienne Rich, "Compulsory Heterosexuality and Lesbian Existence," *Signs*, vol. 5 no. 4 (1980).

18. Germaine Greer has been promoting alternatives to sexual intercourse as a form of birth control for years, and discusses the intriguing thesis that sexual intercourse is dangerous to one's health in *Sex and Destiny: The Politics of Human Fertility* (Toronto: Stoddart, 1984).

19. C. Vance, ed., *Pleasure and Danger: Exploring Female Sexuality* (London: Routledge and Kegan Paul, 1984).

20. See L. Duggan, N. Hunter, and C. Vance, "False Promises," in *Women Against Censorship*. At a meeting of anti-censorship activists held in Toronto in the winter of 1985, Vance promoted the thesis that a single sexually explicit image would repel one third of the viewers, attract one third and leave another third disinterested.

21. See Cedar and Nell, eds., *A Woman's Touch* (Eugene: Womenshare, 1979); Samois Collective, ed., *Coming to Power* (Berkeley: Up, 1981); and Pat Califia, *Macho Sluts* (Boston: Alyson, 1988).

22. See Gayle Rubin, "Talking Sex," in *Pleasure and Danger*, note 19 above. Rubin has taken up the pro-sex banner while repudiating

earlier wonderful work. "The Traffic in Women," in Rayna R. Reiter, ed., *Toward an Anthropology of Women* (New York: Monthly Review, 1976) is a truly brilliant analysis of the way prostitution operates as a cross-cultural phenomenon.

23. See, for example, Judith R. Walkowitz, "Male Vice and Female Virtue: Feminism and the Politics of Prostitution in Nineteenth Century Britain," in A. Snitow, C. Stansell and S. Thompson, eds., *Powers of Desire: The Politics of Sexuality* (New York: Monthly Review, 1983).

24. Lonnie Barbach, *Pleaures: Women Write Erotica* (New York: Doubleday, 1984).

25. Andrea Dworkin, *Right Wing Women* (New York: Perigee, 1982), 53.

26. The study was never published, probably because of this profound flaw.

27. For more on this see Susan G. Cole, "Unmasking the Media," *Forum: The Magazine for Secondary School Educators* vol. 13, no. 4 (December 1987-January 1988); and Cole, "Gender, Sex and Transformation in Popular Music," in *Voices of Feminism: Introduction to Women's Studies* (Toronto: Garamond, forthcoming). For those interested in pursuing media strategies in general, there is a growing body of material. Len Masterman, *Teaching the Media* (London: Comedia, 1985) is considered the basic text. See also *The Resource Book on Media Literacy: Kindergarten through Grade XIII*, referred to in the text.

28. The term is coined by Mariana Valverde and Lorna Weir in "Thrills, Chills and the Lesbian Threat," in *Women Against Censorship*.

29. See Geraldine Finn's magnificently militant "Against Sexual Imagery—Alternative or Otherwise," *Parallelogram* vol. 12 no. 1 (fall 1986). The title speaks for itself. Finn's theory of why pornography's system is impossible to break was developed earlier in "Patriarchy and Pleasure: The Pornographic Eye/I," *Canadian Journal of Political and Social Theory* vol. IX. no. 1 and 2 (winter/spring, 1985).

30. Sheila Jeffreys, *The Spinster and Her Enemies: Feminism and Sexuality 1880-1930* (London: Pandora, 1985).

31. Dworkin, Right Wing Women, 224.

32. Jeffreys made this comment at a conference entitled Sex Liberals and the Attack on Feminism, held in New York, April 2-3, 1987. The conference brought together radical feminists to challenge the sex liberalism we felt was threatening to eclipse feminist attempts to struggle against patriarchal erotic systems. The proceedings of the

conference will be published in the fall of 1989: Dorchen Leidholdt, Janice Raymond eds., *The Sex Liberals and the Attack on Feminism* (New York: Pergamon). Jeffreys' new book *Anticlimax* will be published by Pandora in the spring of 1989.

33. See Califia's *Macho Sluts*, 13.

34. This is the reading I give to Andrea Dworkin's book *Intercourse* (New York: Free Press, 1987). At the New York conference on sex liberalism mentioned in note 32 above, a group operating without the approval of the organizers distributed a pamphlet entitled "Against Sexual Intercourse."

UNIVERSITY OF WOLVERHAMPTON
LEARNING RESOURCES